Educational
Environments
No. 2

Educational
Environments
No. 2

Roger Yee

Visual Reference Publications Inc., New York

Left: Beaman Student Life Center/
Curb Event Center, Tennessee

Design Firm: Earl Swensson Associates

Photography: Robt. Ames Cook, Michael Lewis

Visual Reference Publications Inc.
302 Fifth Avenue
New York, NY 10001

Distributors to the trade in the United States and Canada
Watson-Guptill
770 Broadway
New York, NY 10003

Distributors outside the United States and Canada
HarperCollins International
10 East 53rd Street
New York, NY 10022-5299

Library of Congress Cataloging in Publication Data:
Educational Environments No. 2

Printed in China
ISBN 1-58471-049-7

Book Design: Priscilla Sue Mascia

Contents

Web Directory

Bradley
www.bradleycorp.com

Duracase
ww.duragroup.com

Forbo Flooring
www.forbolinoleumna.com

KI
www.ki.com

SCUP
www.scup.org

Stonhard Floor Systems
www.stonhard.com/edu

Educational Environments Advertisers Invite You to Find Out More About Their Products and Services On-Line.

Right: Cutler Majestic Theatre at Emerson College, Massachusetts

Design firm: Elkus/Manfredi Architects

Bottom right and far right: Tokyo University of Foreign Studies.

Design firm: SWA Group

Introduction

When Barbie™ whined,

"Math Class is Tough!",

Educators told her to shut up— and she listened.

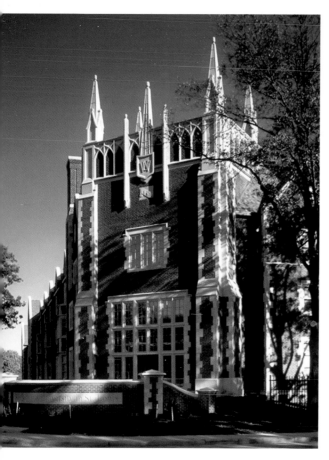

Far left: Washington University, Missouri

Design firm: Mackey Mitchell Associates

Above left: Texas Christian University.

Design firm: Cannon Design

Left: Stanford University, California

Design firm: SWA Group

Toy maker Mattel didn't foresee the coming storm in October 1992 when it gave Teen Talk Barbie™ a voice to declare, "Math class is tough!" While the company pleaded that it was simply expressing the feelings of typical school-age girls, unhappy parents, teachers and professional organizations told the plastic doll to shut up—which she promptly did when Mattel withdrew her two months later. Though there was ample evidence that boys excelled in math and girls did better in verbal related skills, educators made a determined effort to help girls overcome social barriers to mathematics. Sure enough, the respected Trends in International Mathematics and Science Study reported in 1999 that U.S. eighth grade girls were, performing as well in mathematics as boys in their classes, demonstrating education's power to change modern life.

Citizens of developed nations like the United States and its G-7 partners see the value of education all around them. In recent years, however, they have observed how foreign businesses in such rapidly developing nations as India, China and Russia use education to capture not only their manufacturing markets, but their white collar jobs as well. The outsourcing of high-technology work has introduced a new sense of urgency to education. How should Americans school their children and themselves for this brave new world?

No one has answered this question decisively yet. However, the nation's educators, parents and communities are already revising educational philosophies so every child has many new ways to learn, and are working with architects to develop innovative places to make this happen. The striking examples of new educational environments in the following pages, designed by some of the nation's leading architects, often blend time-tested truths with calculated risk-taking to achieve uncommon results. Will they succeed? As a first step, today's schools look friendlier to students than ever—a change Barbie shouldn't find tough to accept.

Roger Yee
Editor

Preface

*O*nce again, the Society for College and University Planning (SCUP) is pleased to introduce Educational Environments No. 2, a compendium of outstanding achievements at institutions of higher learning across the country and around the world. Like the first, this volume gives us a glimpse of the best in new facilities by world class designers: of innovations and emerging trends in design and construction reflective and supportive of changes in instructional delivery modes and places for learning, of breakthroughs in application of new materials and technologies, and of a growing commitment to creating sustainable environments.

SCUP is approaching its 40th year as a leader in comprehensive higher education planning, recognizing and supporting all the elements of planning that contribute to dynamic learning environments. With nearly 5,000 members around the world, SCUP continues to emphasize collegiality and cross-boundary planning among professionals inside and outside of the academy as integral to the quality and vitality of higher education. I am proud to see so many SCUP members among the professional firms showcased in this volume, and to know the many SCUP campus-based members with whom they have collaborated to bring these projects into reality.

The United States and a good portion of the world are bracing for the largest ever influx of elementary, secondary, and traditional aged college students. Coupled with the now continuous need for lifelong learning, higher education is being asked to serve a myriad of learners of all ages, to meet the demands of a vigorous research community, to extend their reach beyond the campus gates deep into their local communities, and indeed to expand around the globe. The projects in this book explore exciting ways to meet these challenges.

At first glance the projects in this volume may appear to be about the physical environment, but upon closer examination, you will sense the potential that they have unleashed for learning at many levels – physical, emotional, cultural, intellectual— and for creating an enduring sense of place that will remain in the memories not only of the students who linger only briefly, but also of the faculty, the staff, and members of the community. You may find models that will give power to your own settings.

SCUP has long been dedicated to bringing the best of planning in all its forms to its membership. It now recommends this volume of *Educational Environments No. 2*, not only to its members, but to all those who care about good design and execution to support that which is most vital to our world—the learning and growth of future generations. As you review this planning and design resource, I am sure that like me, you will be confident that planning for places of learning is in good hands.

L. Carole Wharton
President

Andropogon Associates, Ltd.

10 Shurs Lane
Philadelphia, PA 19127
215.487.0700
215.483.7520 (Fax)
www.andropogon.com

Andropogon Associates, Ltd.

University of Pennsylvania Quadrangle College Houses Philadelphia, Pennsylvania

Since 1751 the school proposed by Benjamin Franklin has admitted students to its 269-acre Philadelphia campus, and generations of students have passed through the prestigious University of Pennsylvania to become accomplished members of society. So it's not surprising that the conversion of the Quadrangle, the historical freshman dormitory designed by Cope and Stewardson in 1886, to a college house system would require a complete overhaul of site infrastructure and comprehensive landscape renovation. The major challenge for the landscape design, which involved Andropogon Associates as landscape architect with EwingCole and John Milner Architects as architects and George Thomas as architectural historian, was to keep facilities operational during school semesters by scheduling reconstruction during strategic 12-week intervals over a four-year period. A revamped pedestrian circulation plan was created to support the new house system, featuring four distinct courtyards at access areas. To overcome long-term flooding problems and intensive recreational use, the design introduced a new integrated storm water management system, stately walkways paved in granite, bluestone and brick, intimate formal gathering spaces and extensive new plantings. Over 250 canopy and understory trees were planted during the land-scape renovation, along with tens of thousands of perennials, ground covers and flowering bulbs, creat-ing a scholar's paradise for 23,243 students and 4,483 faculty.

Andropogon Associates, Ltd.

Oberlin College
Adam Joseph Lewis Center for Environmental Studies
Oberlin, Ohio

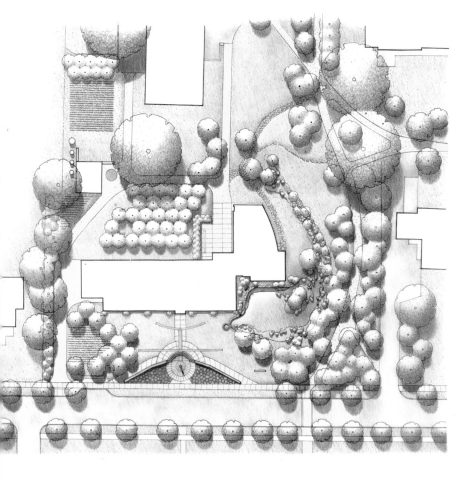

Green design dramatically transcends theory at the new, award-winning Adam Joseph Lewis Center for Environmental Studies at Oberlin College, in Oberlin, Ohio. The building and its landscape serve as a visible model of modern, high-tech, green architecture in their approach to energy, water, materials, landscape and aesthetics. This gives students in Environmental Studies a unique, hands-on learning opportunity. Andropogon Associates, in collaboration with John Lyle, served as landscape architect for the Lewis Center, with William McDonough & Partners as architect. Since a primary design goal has been to create an environment for learning about ecological processes by observation and participation, the landscape design carefully reinforces and augments the natural processes of the site, especially those critical to the atmosphere, the hydrologic regime, plant and animal communities and the soil. The landscape, inspired by the surrounding agricultural region, features a pond that demonstrates "storm water harvesting" and bioremediation, processing storm water runoff. Traditionally the runoff would be diverted to the city's storm water collection system. This places Oberlin, an independent coeducational institution founded in 1833, on the cutting edge of green design.

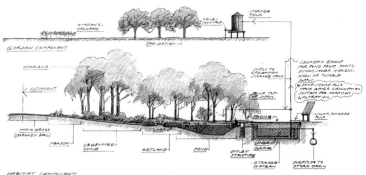

Right: Center with pond in foreground.

Above: Diagram of Habitat component.

Top left: Site plan.

Opposite left: Wetland vegetation.

Photography: Barney Taxel.

12

Andropogon Associates, Ltd.

University of Toronto
Kings College Circle Project
Toronto, Ontario, Canada

A new gateway plants a landmark image in a busy commercial area of Toronto to signal the entry to King's College Road and the historic campus of the University of Toronto. Founded in 1827, it is Canada's largest and most distinguished university. However, there is more to the renovation of the King's College Circle precinct than a formal welcome to the green open spaces of King's College Circle, Hart House Circle, the Back Campus and Philosopher's Walk at its heart. Having developed an open space master plan in 1999, the University commissioned Andropogon Associates to design a schematic plan for the precinct and to implement the first phase of the open space plan. The splendidly revitalized ceremonial spaces, pedestrian walkways, green park spaces and service corridors function in a practical sense. They also introduce a stylish and elegant order as the design standard for the historic campus, and reclaim it for the social life of the University.

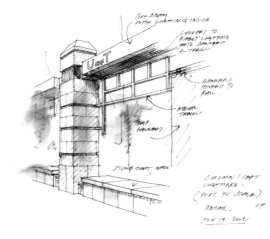

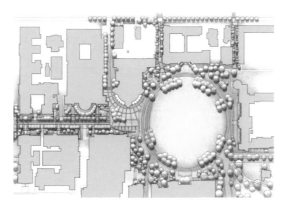

Top: Proposed gateway to historic campus.

Above: Column and trellis detail.

Left: Plan view.

Right: Completed gateway and streetscape.

Photography: Steven Evans Photography.

Illustration: Ronghui-Li, Elias + Associates.

Andropogon Associates, Ltd.

University of North Carolina at Chapel Hill
Environmental Master Plan
Chapel Hill, North Carolina

The University of North Carolina at Chapel Hill continues to evolve. The school founded in 1789 will be a model of sustainable development, having recognized that the health of land and water resources for the campus and surrounding community depends on preserving and restoring these resources. Thus, Andropogon Associates worked with Ayers Saint Gross and the Master Plan team to develop the Environmental Component for the Comprehensive Master Plan. The Environmental Master Plan gives the University strategies to mitigate environmental damage, solve continuing environmental problems and reduce long-term maintenance costs as it develops its two campus areas. The flat, open greens with mature, relic canopy trees, and forested slopes and stream valleys maintain a living heritage for the school.

Top: Site plan for south campus.

Above left: Historic greens of main campus.

Left: Physiography of south campus.

Far left: Environmental structure for entire campus.

Photography: Andropogon Associates, Ltd.

Anshen+Allen Los Angeles

5055 Wilshire Blvd
Los Angeles, CA 90036
323.525.0500
323.525.0955 (Fax)
www.anshen.com

Anshen+Allen Los Angeles

University of California, San Diego
Powell-Focht Bioengineering Building
La Jolla, California

For the University of California, San Diego, the claim that innovation is its tradition is a simple statement of fact. Established four decades ago, UCSD has rapidly become one of the nation's top institutions for higher education and research, as measured by the prestigious organizations that honor it, including the National Science Foundation. The quality of its 23,000 students, and the accomplishments of its faculty members, who include seven Nobel Prize laureates also testify to its accomplishments. The school's dedication is clearly visible in one of the latest additions to its 1,200-acre campus, the handsome, 109,076-square foot, four-story (plus basement) Powell-Focht Bioengineering Building, designed by Anshen+Allen

Los Angeles. Housing the multi-disciplinary research of UCSD's Department of Bioengineering, the new facility represents the first phase of a precinct plan to create an Academic Court on a former playing field adjacent to the massive Jacobs Engineering Building and fronting the Warren Mall, foreground for UCSD's iconic hilltop central library. Inside, faculty and students have two distinct options for research and study. Above the basement's flexible laboratories for joint ventures with private industry and the ground floor's lobby, administration suite,

classrooms and multi-purpose lecture hall, the south wing contains laboratories with support spaces and conference rooms housed in a central zone, and offices located at the ends. The north wing, by contrast, groups the offices

as a suite among the laboratories to foster faculty interaction. Giving faculty and students what they need to excel is what Powell-Focht and UCSD are all about.

Bioengineering Hall
...er Institute of Biomedical Engineering

Opposite: Views of the lecture hall, entry lobby and lounge.

Above: Main entrance.

Right: Laboratory.

Far right: Conference room.

Photography: Tom Bonner, Robert Canfield Photography.

Anshen+Allen Los Angeles

Santa Monica College Library
Santa Monica, California

A proud and energetic two-year community college that opened in 1929 with just 153 students and now serves 25,000 students in over 80 fields of study, Santa Monica College recently asked Anshen+Allen Los Angeles to completely renovate and expand its earthquake-damaged Library. The assignment, repairing the structure, creating a modern and appealing environment for research and study, adding a computer commons and computer laboratory, and making the problematic main entry more visible to passersby on the campus's main pedestrian mall, has produced an award-winning, 98,000-square foot, three-story facility in concrete, steel, glass and wood that has been busy since its reopening.

The reborn Library welcomes students and faculty to book stacks, reader stations, computer commons, bibliographic instructional classroom, archives, copy rooms, technical services and administrative offices in a soaring interior rich with complex forms and spaces, dynamic views, advanced technology and sophisticated lighting. While the computer commons and computer laboratory, housed in a separate, acoustically treated, three-story interior structure sheathed in wood, and the expansive new "front porch" entrance may be the design's most dramatic elements, few empty seats can be seen anywhere in the Library on a typical day.

Top left: Entrance.

Above left: Indoor atrium.

Above: Evening view of exterior.

Right: Curtain wall detail.

Opposite: Computer commons and computer laboratory.

Photography: Tom Bonner.

Anshen+Allen Los Angeles

University of Iowa
Seamans Center-College of Engineering
Iowa City, Iowa

Enlarged by additions over the years, the Seamans Center at the University of Iowa's College of Engineering, in Iowa City, had become internally fragmented and disorienting as well. For this reason, the Center's recent 58,000-square foot renovation and 103,000-square foot expansion sought to establish a new sense of community as well as add new research and teaching laboratories, classrooms, seminar rooms and computer facilities.

Anshen+Allen Los Angeles' striking design succeeds through reorganized circulation and public areas, modernized facilities and building systems, a spacious and open addition that relocates the building's main entrance, and two expansive new program elements, the Student Learning Center and Student Commons, that transform everything around them. As the building's new academic core, the Learning Center extends the renovated library with a majestic, double-height room. Simultaneously, the Commons and its adjacent, five-story atrium create a luminous new social focal point, flooded in daylight.

Top right: Laboratory.

Above left: Student Learning Center.

Above right: Computer Bar.

Left: Addition and entrance.

Opposite: Student Commons and atrium.

Photography: Assassi Productions.

Executive Architect: Neumann Monson PC Architects

Anshen+Allen Los Angeles

University of Washington
Bioengineering and Genome Sciences Building
Seattle, Washington

The University of Washington knows how to operate without wasting time or money. Indeed, the school started as the Territorial University of Washington in 1861, and closed several times in its infancy for lack of funds. When the new, 265,000-square foot, eight-level (five above grade) Bioengineering and Genome Sciences Building, designed by Anshen+Allen Los Angeles, is completed on its Seattle campus, the project will conclude a fast schedule that saw construction begin before drawings were finished. The new building sustains a complex environment nonetheless, fulfilling an intensive program on a limited site with research and teaching laboratories, vivarium, faculty offices, 200-seat auditorium, 200-seat café and support space—all for two separate departments in two linked buildings. Clear design concepts, such as locating wet laboratories on the west side of block offices and dry computational laboratories on the east side, placing public and teaching spaces on lower floors that touch grade as the site slopes to water, and sheathing the building with terra cotta, glass and sun shades, will keep the development moving towards opening day.

Above left: Site plan.

Top and above right: Details of the facades.

Illustration: Anshen+Allen Los Angeles.

ARC/Architectural Resources Cambridge, Inc.

140 Mount Auburn Street
Cambridge, MA 02138
617.547.2200
617.547.7222(Fax)
www.arcusa.com

ARC/Architectural Resources Cambridge, Inc.

ARC/Architectural Resources Cambridge, Inc.

Harvard Medical School
New Research Building
Boston, Massachusetts

Above left: Main elevation looking toward auditorium & conference center.

Above right: Westwing laboratory tower, with Blackfan Street entry at newly created Plaza.

Right: Typical open laboratory.

Opposite: Main lobby facing Avenue Louis Pasteur.

Photography: Jeff Goldberg/ ESTO Photographics.

The education of a medical student in late 18th-century America would seem astonishingly incomplete to today's physician. A semester or two of formal lectures were followed by an apprenticeship to a practicing physician for several years. Since academic preparation was not required, written exams were not mandatory, and little clinical training was given in the absence of teaching hospitals. Such were the circumstances on September 19, 1782, when Harvard College established its Medical School in Cambridge, Massachusetts with three professors and a handful of students. From this humble beginning, Harvard Medical School would become one of the world's preeminent institutions in medical education and research, with nearly 8,000 faculty members, a student body of 650 in the MD program, 477 in the PhD program, and 132 in the joint MD-PhD programs, 17 affiliated teaching hospitals and 25 centers, divisions and institutes. Among the latest milestones in the School's distinguished career is the opening of the New Research Building designed by ARC/Architectural Resources Cambridge, a 740,000-square foot, 10-story, glass-sheathed structure, that is Harvard's largest building built to date. What highlights this handsome facility beyond its sheer size and bold aesthetic is its commitment to

ARC/Architectural Resources Cambridge, Inc.

medical advancement through greater scientific collaboration. "By having hospital-based and school-based faculty working side-by-side in this new environment, biomedical opportunities will emerge and be taken more quickly from laboratory to bedside," noted Joseph Martin, dean of the Medical School, at the dedication ceremony. The concept of shared spaces goes beyond the laboratories to include common and group discussion areas, conference and meeting rooms, and lounges located throughout the structure, which enfold and connect to the existing, 10-story Harvard Institutes of Medicine. There are three basic components: a four-story structure along Avenue Louis Pasteur housing a 500-seat auditorium and conference center, a 10-story research tower set back from the street, and a below-grade parking garage providing 559 parking spaces. While the building is essentially a biomedical research facility, its exceptional environment turns formal and casual encounters of physicians and scientists into everyday occurrences by supporting its shared spaces with such amenities as interior courtyards, bridges, breakout areas, a café and landscaping. Lawrence Summers, president of Harvard University, hailed the concept driving its design by predicting, "Many people may never know about this building decades from now, but there will be tens of thousands of them who will live longer lives of great joy because of it."

Above left: Dusk view of New Research Building and Harvard Institutes of Medicine, seen at left rear.

Left: Canopy at main entrance.

Right: The 500-seat auditorium.

Below: Main entry atrium stair to concourse.

ARC/Architectural Resources Cambridge, Inc.

Tufts University
Jaharis Family Center for Biomedical and Nutrition Sciences
Boston, Massachusetts

Right: Main lobby.

Below: The 200-seat interactive teleconferencing auditorium.

Opposite: Nine-story Harrison Avenue elevation.

Photography: Warren Patterson.

In a perceptive commentary about the new, 180,000-square foot, nine-story Jaharis Family Center for Biomedical and Nutrition Sciences at Tufts University's Boston campus, Tufts president Lawrence Bacow pointed out, "Increasingly, some of the most important questions in science lie at the intersection of disciplines. Our ability to generate new knowledge will depend on our capacity to focus the resources of basic science, clinical medicine and nutrition on some of the great questions in medicine, such as the origins of cancer." The brick, aluminum and glass structure, designed by ARC/Architectural Resources Cambridge, encourages basic scientists, clinical researchers, nutritionists, and students and their programs from three schools at Tufts, including the School of Medicine, Sackler School of Graduate Biomedical Sciences and Gerald J. and Dorothy R. Friedman School of Nutrition Science, to work together within the world's first collaborative biomedical and nutrition research center. While research laboratories dominate the interiors, they are accompanied by administrative and faculty offices, classrooms, a 200-seat auditorium and indoor and outdoor café areas to encourage and help foster interaction. The auditorium provides a setting for outreach to scientists and researchers in related fields throughout the world. The laboratory floors represent the facility's most distinctive

ARC/Architectural Resources Cambridge, Inc.

feature housing a mix of people working on related research. Comprised of three lateral zones, including generic open laboratories for bench work, adjacent laboratory support spaces and office suites, each laboratory floor allows researchers to expand or shrink individual laboratories as needed, knowing their shared support spaces are sized to fit the laboratory bench building module and can be altered with minimal disruption. A suggestion of the complex activities housed on these laboratory floors can be seen in the list of occupants, with the Friedman School occupying the 1st floor

and portions of the 2nd, the Community Health/ Infectious Disease program of the School of Medicine occupying the remainder of the 2nd floor and the School of Medicine's Department of Pathology occupying the 5th, 8th and 9th floors. The remaining 3rd, 4th, 6th and 7th floors house laboratories of faculty from parts of the School of Medicine's basic science departments of Physiology, Biochemistry, Anatomy and Cell Biology, Molecular Biology and Microbiology, and Pharmacology. With the help of major donor and pharmaceutical industry leader Michael Jaharis and his family, the Center now offers

the promise of vital medical discoveries made possible by its unique organization.

Above: Detail of brick, aluminum and glass curtain-wall.

Top left: Café.

Upper left: Private office and conference area.

Left: Auditorium presentation area with retractable monitors.

Lower left: Typical generic laboratory bench layout.

Ayers/Saint/Gross

Architects + Planners

1040 Hull Street
Suite 100
410.347.8500
410.347.8519 (Fax)

800 Eye Street NW
Suite 600
Washington, DC 20001
202.628.1033
202.628.1034 (Fax)

214 E. Roosevelt St.
South Studio
Phoenix, AZ 85004
602.716.9700   www.asg-architects.com
602.712.1882   jwheeler@asg-architects.com

Ayers/Saint/Gross

Ayers/Saint/Gross

Haverford College
Koshland Integrated Natural Sciences Center
Haverford, Pennsylvania

How do you bring seven science departments under one roof to promote collaborative learning and research? For Haverford College, a coeducational undergraduate liberal arts college founded in 1833 by the Religious Society of Friends (Quakers), the effort began with close cooperation among faculty members representing the departments, the president, provost and other college officers, and the project team from Ayers/Saint/Gross. Consequently, the chemistry, physics, astronomy, computer science, mathematics, biology and psychology departments are now accommodated in award-winning new and renovated facilities in the 120,000-square foot, three-story Marian E. Koshland Integrated Natural Sciences Center, and 18,000-square foot renovation of Sharpless

and Hilles Halls. The benefits to Haverford go beyond the state-of-the-art teaching and research laboratories, classrooms, offices, seminar rooms, conference rooms, interactive lounges and library. The Koshland Center is aligned with adjacent buildings to function as a gateway between the upper and lower sections of the campus, with the new structure's circular atrium acting as the focal point. Commenting about the development, Norman Ricker, Jr., director of physical plant, gratefully concludes, "As a cost-saving measure, we combined stone with stucco and everyone agrees we have a more interesting exterior as a result."

Above: Rotunda.

Left: View towards Sharpless Hall.

Far left: Library.

Opposite: Exterior and entrance to rotunda.

Photography: Alan Karchmer

Ayers/Saint/Gross

Messiah College
Boyer Hall Academic Building
Grantham, Pennsylvania

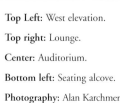

Now gracing the campus of Messiah College, a Christian institution founded in 1909 by the Brethren in Christ Church, is Boyer Hall, a 98,170-square foot, four-story academic building designed by Ayers/Saint/Gross. It is a glowing testimony to the power of architecture to bestow meaning as well as utility. The brick-clad structure consists of 22 general use classrooms, a 140-seat auditorium/ film studio, specialized classrooms for teacher education, language laboratory, department resource rooms, administrative office suite, writing/learning centers, behavioral science interview and counseling rooms, and offices for 45 percent of the College's faculty. As traditional as Boyer Hall appears, its technology is state-of-the-art, so all classrooms have audiovisual and telecommunications cabling and infrastructure. Yet students and the faculty are finding that Boyer Hall also forms vital connections to campus life. They utilize its steeply sloping site as a gateway from the campus green to playing fields beyond the Yellow Breeches River and use its atrium as a public passageway that has become a favorite gathering place.

Top Left: West elevation.

Top right: Lounge.

Center: Auditorium.

Bottom left: Seating alcove.

Photography: Alan Karchmer

Ayers/Saint/Gross

University of Delaware
Center for the Arts
Newark, Delaware

Another step in the evolution of the University of Delaware from its founding as a small private academy in 1743 to a major university with more than 16,000 under-graduates and nearly 3,000 graduate students will soon be taken. The completion of the 93,000-square foot Center for the Arts will accompany an already fin-ished 220,000-square foot parking garage, both designed by Ayers/Saint/Gross. The Center will support the instructional needs of the University's theater and music depart-ments at the same time it provides a multi-level performing arts facility for campus and community events. The extensive accommodations, including a 450-seat proscenium theater, 200-seat recital hall, 300-seat music rehearsal hall, theater rehearsal room, 32 music practice rooms and administrative office spaces, will satisfy a wide range of performers and audiences. And there will be room for an encore: a future 42,000-square foot, 800-seat concert hall.

Top: Amstel Avenue elevation.

Left: Lobby.

Above right: Orchestra rehearsal hall.

Right: Recital hall.

Illustration and 3-D visualization: Ayers/Saint/Gross.

Ayers/Saint/Gross

Emory University
Nell Hodgson Woodruff School of Nursing
Atlanta, Georgia

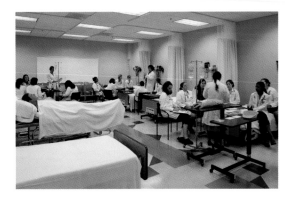

Top: The School's two linked structures.

Center: Main entrance.

Above right: Case study room.

Photography: Gary Knight.

Design Architect: Ayers/Saint/Gross

Executive Architect: Stang & Newman, Inc.

As one of the respected professional schools at Atlanta's Emory University, the Nell Hodgson Woodruff School of Nursing is appropriately located along the Clifton Corridor. The site includes the U.S. Centers for Disease Control and Prevention and the American Cancer Society, in the tree-lined suburban neighborhood of Druid Hills. The School of Nursing is a leader in preparing nurses for beginning and advanced practice. The latest sign of its leadership is its new 99,000-square foot home, designed by Ayers/Saint/Gross. Reflecting the complex role of nurses in today's medical profession, the new facility comprises two linked structures, a larger five-story building containing administrative and faculty offices, instructional and skills laboratories, ancillary spaces, and a smaller, three-story building, the teaching pavilion, housing a large auditorium, case study rooms and large classrooms. The School forms a prominent gateway at the northern boundary of the Emory campus and is connected to the School of Public Health. It's a fresh start in more ways than one, since it is one of the first buildings designed under master plan guidelines created by Ayers/ Saint/Gross in 1998.

Ayers/Saint/Gross

University of Virginia
Darden Graduate School of Business Administration
Charlottesville, Virginia

Top above: Darden Center and Saunders Hall.

Above: Auditorium.

Below right: Dining room.

Photography: Alan Karchmer.

Thomas Jefferson lived 169 years too soon to witness the birth of the Darden Graduate School of Business Administration at the University of Virginia in Charlottesville. However, the influence of the third President of the United States, who founded the University in 1819, is evident in the development of the School through a 210,000-square foot Phase I in 1995 and 308,000-square foot Phase II in 2003. To build a proper facility for a professional school seeking to "better

society by developing leaders in the world of practical affairs," the University assembled a project team that included Ayers/Saint/Gross as executive architect for Phase I and design and managing architect for Phase II, along with Robert A.M. Stern as design architect for Phase I and Glave Homes as associate architect for Phase II. The noble Jeffersonian architecture, encompassing auditoriums, tiered classrooms, group study rooms, offices, dining facilities, library

and parking garage in connected buildings on an 18-acre site, would surely have pleased Jefferson, a gifted architect in his own right.

Ayers/Saint/Gross

Virginia Commonwealth University
Life Sciences Center
Richmond, Virginia

Left Top: Street elevation.

Above: Atrium.

Left Below: Science quadrangle.

Photography: Alan Karchmer.

A university with more than 26,000 students is virtually impossible to ignore in the downtown district of any community. Consequently, the new, 128,500-square foot, four-story Life Sciences Center on one of Virginia Commonwealth University's two downtown Richmond campuses takes a forthright approach to siting. Its thoughtful urban design adds a contemporary interpretation of Georgian architecture to the cityscape, defines a science quadrangle, and fosters interaction among the sciences. Designed by Ayers/Saint/Gross as design associate, Sverdrup Facilities as architect of record, and GPR Planners Collaborative as laboratory planner, the center offers state-of-the-art space that can adapt to changing methodology and technology. Research and teaching laboratories, classrooms, lecture halls, case study rooms, seminar classrooms, offices and support space will enhance downtown Richmond throughout each academic year.

Bergmeyer Associates, Inc.

286 Congress Street
Boston, MA 02210
617.542.1025
617.338.6897 (Fax)
www.bergmeyer.com

Bergmeyer Associates, Inc.

Harvard University
Center for the Study of World Religions
Cambridge, Massachusetts

Upper left: Corridor.

Upper right: Lounge.

Above: Library.

Opposite: Stairwell.

Photography: Greg Premru.

In the late 1950's esteemed architect Josep Luis Sert, director of Harvard University's Graduate School of Design, was asked to design the 22,000-square foot Center for the Study of World Religions on a site in Cambridge, Massachusetts across the street from its parent institution, Harvard Divinity School. He gave visual expression to the Center's desire for autonomy by creating a classic Modernist concrete and glass structure whose U-shaped plan turned its back on the School. When the Center opened three years later in 1960, it included living quarters for the director and his family and for fellows and their families, along with shared space where they could create a community. However, the passing of time has shifted the Center's outlook towards interaction. On the wish list for the recent renovation by Bergmeyer, the staff included a new lobby with reception area and elevator, new office facilities, the conversion of underutilized, existing apartments into collaborative research space, the creation of a more useful seminar/ lecture space with adjoining kitchen and fellows' study, the updating of existing public areas, and the upgrading of existing building systems to contemporary standards.

Not surprisingly, the staff also requested that the renovation be respectful of Sert's original International Style creation. Now that the work has been completed, people are seen lingering in the refurbished spaces to share their ideas and enjoy the environment, renewing the vitality that Sert's original design brought in the Center four decades ago.

Bergmeyer Associates, Inc.

Washington and Lee University
The John W. Elrod University Commons
Lexington, Virginia

Venerable as the 80,000-square foot, three-story, Neoclassical John W. Elrod University Commons appears, majestically overlooking Woods Creek on the Washington and Lee University campus in Lexington, Virginia, its story reaches forward and backward in time. The new facility promotes a future of greater unity between the school's commuter students and fraternity and sorority members, as much as it honors a past that includes its founding in 1749 and stewardship under General Robert E. Lee, who became its president in 1865. Accordingly, the architects of the Commons, VMDO Architects (shell and core) and Bergmeyer (programming and interiors), developed a contemporary environment with traditional motifs to consolidate student-oriented organizations and activities scattered throughout the campus. Now both commuters and "Greeks" enjoy the Commons for its marketplace-style dining facility and café, formal lounge for students, visiting parents and staff, cinema, meeting rooms, student organizations and career development offices.

Top: Exterior.

Above far left: Bookstore.

Above left: Cinema.

Far left: Café.

Left: Dining.

Opposite: Servery.

Photography: Prakash Patel

Bergmeyer Associates, Inc.

Northeastern University
780 Columbus Avenue
Boston, Massachusetts

Visitors to Boston's Northeastern University, a private university noted for its practice-oriented education, might never suspect that a school with 14,492 undergraduates and 2,232 graduate students began as the "Department of Law of the Boston YMCA" in 1898 with "an eraser and two sticks of chalk." Resourcefulness is a hallmark of Northeastern, and the creation of 780 Columbus Avenue, a new, 40,000-square foot, five-story, 117-bed residence hall, designed by Bergmeyer, shows why. The facility was converted from a former warehouse to meet pressing housing needs in only 10 months. The tight schedule and the project entailed installing entirely new building systems, renovating the existing facades, adding a fifth floor and installing the living units. Close communication and coordination among Northeastern, the design team and the general contractor made "117 beds in 117 days" a reality. Yet the haste is hardly apparent inside the new residence. Students vie for the living units, which exploit the structure's tall windows and floor-to-floor height to establish an urban, loft-like feeling with raised sleeping platforms sharing light from the living room windows.

Bergmeyer Associates, Inc.

Salem State College
Central Campus Residence Hall
Salem, Massachusetts

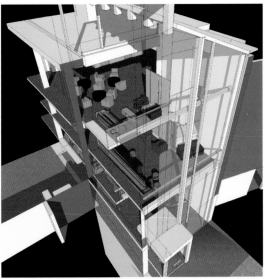

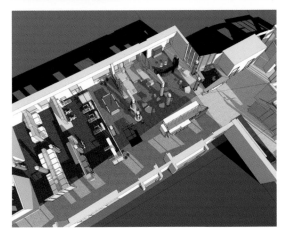

A new, 142,000-square foot, four-story, 458-bed Residence Hall, designed by Bergmeyer Associates, marks the latest milestone in Salem State College's evolution as a thriving, coeducational institution in Salem, Massachusetts that opened in 1854. The new Residence Hall, planned with students and faculty, will create 75 six-person, apartment-style student suites, one residential staff unit, two graduate assistant studios and two faculty apartments, and act as a focal point of the Central Campus. To nurture an academic community within its walls, the facility will incorporate study areas, a well-equipped seminar room, and an extensive first-floor lounge offering fitness, laundry, pool tables and other games, as well as adjacent academic and administrative offices. Outside, the building will use its long, low form and H-shaped layout to frame views of an open green lawn, the largest at Salem State, to the west, and a tidal salt marsh and the Forest River to the east. Students in the first-floor lounge will be able to look in both directions to sense the College's place in the world, even as the building's Georgian brick-work evokes the heritage of historic Salem, founded in 1626, and its modern architecture looks ahead to the town's fourth century.

Bialosky + Partners Architects

2775 South Moreland Blvd.
Cleveland, OH 44120
216.752.8750
216.752.9437 (Fax)

81 Walker Street
New York, NY 10013
212.941.1390
212.941.9995 (Fax)
www.bialosky.com

Bialosky + Partners Architects

Bialosky + Partners Architects

Muskingum College
Caldwell Hall
New Concord, Ohio

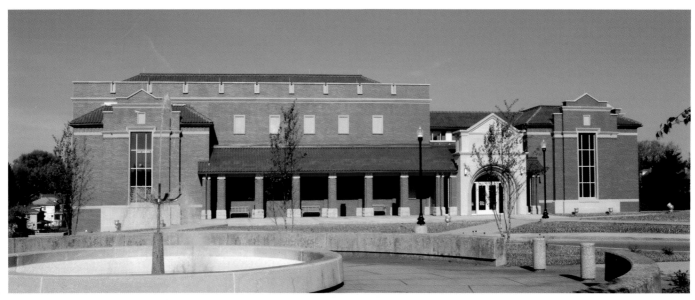

Top: East Facade.

Above: TV Classroom.

Opposite above: Rehearsal Hall & Main Entry.

Opposite right: Theater.

Photography: Scott Pease.

Muskingum College, founded in 1837 in New Concord, Ohio, recently achieved a long-cherished dream by completing Caldwell Hall, its new 32,000-square-foot, 3-level communication arts and theatre building, designed by Bialosky + Partners. The design unites speech, theater, electronic journalism and graphic design under one roof for the 1,600 undergraduate students of this four-year liberal arts college. An ambitious structure whose "Muskingum"-style architecture houses state-of-the-art facilities, Caldwell Hall includes a 250-seat theater, which can be used for either proscenium or in-the-round productions, a rehearsal hall, the WMCO radio studios, and a TV studio. The building also contains the TV and radio production laboratories, set and costume laboratories, classrooms, gallery, and faculty offices. The building's exterior materials include brick and roof tiles made within sixty miles of the College. Additionally, its sensitive placement on a steeply sloping site enables it to have entrances at grade for all three floors and creates with Montgomery Hall and the Library a visitor-friendly entry court first envisioned in a 1920's campus master plan. Harold Burlingame, chairman of the College's Board of Trustees, observes that Caldwell Hall "honors our distinguished legacy in communication and provides our faculty with the tools to help our students strengthen this legacy for the future."

Bialosky + Partners Architects

University of Akron
Institute for Global Business
Akron, Ohio

The University of Akron commissioned the team of Bialosky + Partners and Mont Alto Architecture (a joint venture), to realize their vision for a new signature facility to reinforce the University's presence as a leader in the world's business community. The resulting series of design studies for the Institute of Global Business draw connections between the campus's major east-west pedestrian artery and The City of Akron's Downtown Business district. The final design scheme visually connects the University with Akron's business district, illustrating the real world connection between academia and the global business community. Ted Curtis, Vice President of Capital Planning and Facility Management at the University of Akron reports, "The present design has resulted in a very dynamic, bold and concise statement which will reflect the far-reaching aspects of the global business community." In 2003, the joint venture received authorization to proceed with completing the 55,700-square-foot, five-story new home for the Institute. Designed with an eye towards the future, this contemporary building is fully equipped for networking, distance learning and data mining. The new facility is also flexible in layout for changes in teaching and technology trends and designed to foster interactive and collaborative learning. The Institute for Global Business is clad in a tri-color pre-cast concrete shell with aluminum and glass fenestrations that encircle a soaring, four-story glass atrium. The building incorporates classrooms, study areas, a business library and trading room as well as staff offices and an executive training facility. The Institute will be the new home for the Fisher Institute for Professional Selling, The Fitzgerald Institute for Entrepreneurial Studies and the Center for Organizational Development.

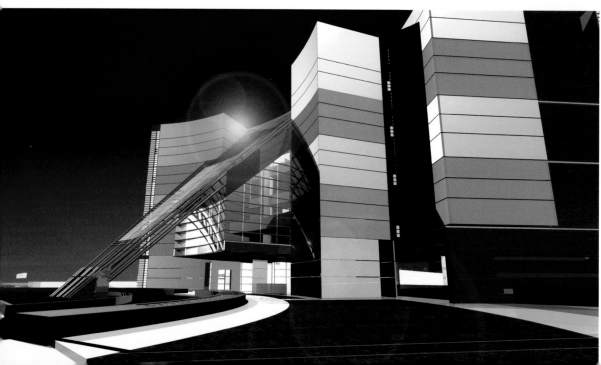

BSA LifeStructures

9635 Counselors Row
Indianapolis, IN 46240
317.819.7878
317.819.7288 (Fax)
www.bsalifestructures.com

440 North Wells Street
Suite 410
Chicago, IL 60610
312.324.5600
312.324.5699 (Fax)

6101 Carnegie Boulevard
Suite 105
Charlotte, NC 28209
704.554.0808
704.553.0055 (Fax)

BSA LifeStructures

Indiana University Kokomo
Virgil and Elizabeth Hunt Hall
Kokomo, Indiana

Above: Main facade facing campus quadrangle.

Left: Curtain wall detail at west entry facade.

Below: Main entrance lobby.

Opposite: North bay window and seating area.

Photography: Scott McDonald /Hedrich Blessing, Steve Richardson.

Fostering interaction between faculty and students was the main goal for the new, 79,000-square foot, two-story Virgil and Elizabeth Hunt Hall at Indiana University Kokomo. Designed by BSA LifeStructures, the interior of the science and mathematics building encourages people to congregate in common or "soft" spaces. There, students and faculty can sit, relax and converse just steps from teaching spaces. The building includes laboratories for research, biology, chemistry, physics, geology, mathematics, information systems and allied health, as well as classrooms, advanced technology auditorium, faculty offices and support space. The thought of bringing people together would have gratified Virgil Hunt, a founder of the Kokomo campus in 1945.

(William and Nancy Hunt, his son and daughter-in-law, made the single largest donation in the University's history to support the Hall.) The architectural impact is dramatic, ranging from the two-story entrance lobby and central monumental stair to the second floor lounges and glass-paneled doors with views into laboratories. Large windows on the north side of the building, overlook tree-lined Kokomo Creek. Dr. Robert Roales, assistant dean of the School of Allied Health Services, declares, "Along with our programs, new equipment and excellent faculty, this facility now makes IU Kokomo a top choice for any student looking for a high-quality science education."

BSA LifeStructures

Wabash College
Detchon Center for Modern Languages and International Studies
Crawfordsville, Indiana

Left: International Hall.

Below left: Reading room.

Below right: New west elevation.

Opposite: New entry/elevator tower.

Photography: Dan Francis/ Mardan Photography.

As anyone knows on the 55-acre campus of Wabash College, in Crawfordsville, Indiana, Yandes Hall was built to last. Constructed in 1891, the brick-and-limestone building was the college library for 67 years. An art gallery, 100-seat stage, fine arts studio, office and classroom space for the German, French and Spanish departments, foreign language laboratory, Humanities Center and a college FM radio broadcasting studio were added along the way. Yet a century later, Yandes Hall faced demolition until the Board of Trustees agreed to expand and convert the Georgian-style edifice into the new, 26,000-square foot, two-story Detchon Center for Modern Languages and International Studies. BSA LifeStructures transformed the original library and art studios into the laboratory and classrooms and incorporated an 8,000-square-foot addition. Detchon Center boasts International Hall, a renovated, two-story space for receptions, dinners, lectures and presentations. Also added was a new entry/ elevator tower that looks as timeless as anything else at this liberal arts college for 860 men founded in 1832.

BSA LifeStructures

Landsbaum Center for Health Education
Terre Haute, Indiana

Right: Main entry.

Below left: Public/teaching clinic.

Below right: Lecture hall.

Opposite: Atrium rotunda.

Photography: Greg Murphey.

A shared vision in education inspired the new, 34,000-square foot, two-story Landsbaum Center for Health Education in Terre Haute, Indiana. The building has become a national model for collaboration. Designed by BSA LifeStructures, the facility unites education programs to train nurses, medical students and family practice residents from Indiana University School of Medicine, Indiana State University College of Nursing and Union Hospital's Midwest Center for Rural Health for careers in rural, underserved communities. The state-of-the-art facility allows them to collaborate and to share facilities and technology such as medical simulators. Within this versatile environment, students and faculty have access to such well equipped and attractive components as a 150-seat lecture hall, classrooms, conference rooms, public/teaching clinic, student team rooms, offices and a circular central lobby. "I love this building. It's incredibly well designed," says Dr. James R. Buechler, director of the Midwest Center for Rural Health. "Usually, after you get into a new building, you think of all the things you wish you'd done differently. I can't say that about this building."

BSA LifeStructures

Purdue University
Colby Fitness Center in the Recreational Sports Center
West Lafayette, Indiana

Whether the aging of Baby Boomers or the rise of health care costs is awakening Americans to the advantages of wellness over intervention, fitness programs now command enough respect across the nation to justify new facilities. One such facility is the new, 19,000-square-foot Colby Fitness Center, on the lower level of Purdue University's

Recreational Sports Center, designed by BSA LifeStructures. The Colby Fitness Center, honoring benefactors Ken and Linda Colby, features over 190 pieces of cardiovascular and strength training equipment, as well as such amenities as 17 TVs, a stereo system with AM/FM headsets, central air conditioning and full ele-

vator access to the entire RSC. Though it occupies a 1950s space with structural limitations, the new design overcomes this obstacle with a multi-level ceiling grid and an opening to the ground floor above that brings in light and connects the facility to the other RSC activities. With faculty, staff and students making more

than 850,000 visits to the Recreational Sports Center each year, the Colby Fitness Center should quicken the pulse of the Purdue community in West Lafayette, Indiana before long.

Upper left: Central control station.

Above left: Cardiovascular workout area.

Above right: Two-story space with balcony.

Photography: Greg Murphey.

Burt Hill Kosar Rittelmann Associates

270 Congress Street
Boston, MA 02210
617.423.4252

400 Morgan Center
101 East Diamond Street
Butler, PA 16001
724.285.476

1 Chagrin Highlands
2000 Auburn Drive
Suite 200
Beachwood, OH 44122
216.378.7840

Apartment No. 604
Block A2, Gulf Tower
Oud Metha
Dubai,UAE
+971 4 3344887

1735 Market Street
53rd Floor
Philadelphia, PA 19103
215.751.2900

650 Smithfield Street
Pittsburgh, PA 15222
412.394.7000
www.burthill.com

Burt Hill Kosar Rittelmann Associates

University of Connecticut
Information Technology Engineering Building
Storrs, Connecticut

Below left: Main elevation.

Right: Atrium and staircase.

Opposite lower left: Lecture hall.

Opposite lower right: Student interactive space.

Photography: Woodruff Brown.

Halfway into a 20-year, $2.8 billion upgrade of six campuses, the University of Connecticut has traveled far from its founding as Storrs Agricultural School in 1881. One of the newest facilities on the main campus at Storrs that reinforces UConn's ranking among America's top 25 public research universities is the 115,700-square foot, five-level Information Technology Engineering Building for the School of Engineering, designed by Burt Hill Kosar Rittelmann Associates. Flanked by the Homer Babbidge Library and Business Administration Building, the ITE Building strengthens the heart of the campus by emphasizing its planning grid and houses the departments of Electrical & Computer Engineering and Computer Science & Engineering in state-of-the-art accommodations. The building's functional spaces—including research and teaching laboratories, classrooms, administrative and faculty offices, executive conference room and faculty lounge even include a touch of drama. While the exterior blends with the campus, the interior revolves around a dramatic, open atrium and staircase that future engineers need no lessons to enjoy.

Burt Hill Kosar Rittelmann Associates

Hiram College
Gerstacker Science Hall
Hiram, Ohio

Left: Main entrance and portico.

Right: Meeting space.

Lower left: Library.

Bottom left: Laboratory.

Photography: Ed Massery.

You don't have to be big to make a difference in education. Hiram College, located in the Village of Hiram, Ohio, is proud that its 900 students come from 26 states and 23 foreign countries, that 31 percent of incoming first-year students are in the top 10 percent of their class and that 95 percent of its 73 full-time faculty members hold the Ph.D. or other terminal degree in their field. The red brick buildings that populate its 110-acre campus are chosen with the same pride and care, as typified by the new, 31,500-square foot, four-story Gerstacker Science Hall, designed by Burt Hill Kosar Rittelmann Associates. Gerstacker Hall satisfies current needs through its teaching and research laboratories, faculty offices, library/meeting space, computer laboratory and general classroom. Looking ahead, the facility will also accommodate future phases and an eventual link to Colton Hall, the oldest building on campus. In a timeless gesture, its ground floor portico extends a warm welcome to the Village of Hiram.

Burt Hill Kosar Rittelmann Associates

Saint Joseph's University
Mandeville Hall, School of Business Administration
Philadelphia, Pennsylvania

Left: Multi-tiered classroom.

Right: Main entrance.

Below left: Front elevation.

Below right: Resource center.

Photography: Tom Crane.

Determined to lead the integration of business and technology, Saint Joseph's University has entered the 21st century with the intellectual rigor that guided its 1851 founding in Philadelphia by the Society of Jesus. The university challenges its 6,500 students to exceed their highest ambitions, fostering the mature development of values, and deepening a desire to help shape the world plus a willingness to employ modern technology. The University's belief is eloquently expressed in the new, 90,000-square foot, four-level Mandeville Hall for the School of Business Administration, designed by Burt Hill Kosar Rittelmann Associates. Mandeville Hall's program is as demanding as its technology, since the Collegiate Gothic-style building includes multi-tiered classrooms, standard classrooms, conference/ seminar rooms, moot boardrooms, faculty department suites, resource center, computer classroom, test kitchen/ tasting room, retail technology laboratory, observation room, auditorium/lecture hall, dining room and warming kitchen. But there's more than meets the eye: fiber optic cabling, multi-media systems and wiring for remote control operations. At Mandeville Hall's dedication ceremony, University president Rev. Nicholas S. Rashford, S.J. declared, "We have guaranteed that Saint Joseph's University students will receive the best education possible for many years to come."

Burt Hill Kosar Rittelmann Associates

Carnegie Mellon University
Doherty Hall - Interdisciplinary Science Laboratories
Pittsburgh, Pennsylvania

Is it possible to have an inviting and collaborative university laboratory where as many student work stations as possible can be accommodated, aisle space promotes student comfort and instrumentation rolling on mobile carts, chemicals are safely transported inside and outside, and the amount of natural light reaching deep inside is maximized? The answer is a resounding yes at least for students using the new, 47,000-square foot addition and 56,000-square foot renovation at Carnegie Mellon University's Doherty Hall, Interdisciplinary Science Laboratories, in Pittsburgh, designed by Burt Hill Kosar Rittelmann Associates. To achieve these goals, the design incorporates such features as major mechanical shafts and ductwork lining one edge of the addition. This provides unobstructed laboratory floor plates across the existing and new structures, laboratory casework and fumehoods positioned to aid student experimentation team clusters with instrumentation parking, chemical storage/handling spaces and major mechanical and electrical spaces gathered at the base of the building for service and accessibility (the main exhaust is at the top). New elevators facilitate the safe transportation of chemicals and instrumentation to laboratories with no routes through public corridors. Abundant windows for daylight and views connect the work within the building to the world it will surely change.

Above: Exterior at night.

Far left: Team cluster area in laboratory.

Left: Open staircase.

Lower far left: Laboratory window wall.

Lower left: Fumehood.

Photography: Ed Massery, Jeff Swensen.

Cannon Design

2170 Whitehaven Road
Grand Island, NY 14072
716.773.6800
716.773.5909 (Fax)
www.cannondesign.com

Cannon Design

Cannon Design

University of California, Berkeley
Centralized Dining &
Student Services Building
Berkeley, California

Distinguished architecture has graced the University of California, Berkeley's 1,232-acre campus since the early 20th century, when benefactor Phoebe Apperson Hearst promoted an international competition soliciting architectural plans for the campus. The tradition continues with the new, 90,000-square foot, three-story Centralized Dining & Student Services Building, designed by Cannon Design. Through its handsome contemporary form, the building honors its architectural heritage, acknowledging the topography of the Berkeley Hills and such

Top right: Main entrance.

Above left: Student Services wing.

Above right: Dining wing.

Opposite: Dining in evening view.

Photography: Tim Griffin, John Edward Linden Photography.

neighbors as the historic, Shingle-style Anna Head School and Bernard Maybeck's great Christian Science Church. Adopting a sustainable approach lets the design maximize the use of daylight and minimize the need for applied decoration. Polished concrete floors, plaster walls, and acoustical ceilings establish a simple look that is durable and easy to maintain. And consolidating facilities once scattered about the campus enables the building to provide student services in a convenient location that is responsive and appropriate to its neighborhood.

Cannon Design

Sabanci University
Istanbul, Turkey

The work of Sinan, imperial architect of the Ottoman Empire, inspired the design of Sabanci University's new, award-winning 1.8 million-square foot campus in Istanbul, Turkey, designed by Cannon Design. The hallmarks of Sinan's design vocabulary have been visibly incorporated into facilities equipped to compete with their most technologically advanced counterparts in universities worldwide. Constructed over a five-year period, the University will serve an ultimate enrollment of 3,000 students in engineering, management, arts, social sciences and language arts. Consistent with the Master Plan, also created by Cannon Design, there are three distinct zones on campus--an academic core, a sports and recreation area, and a housing/ residential village, each infused with a distinct character that imparts variety to the University's suburban environment. With a 300,000-volume library, one of the largest in Turkey, already operating as the symbolic center of the University and the hub of campus life, a business school offering courses modeled after Harvard Business School's case study curriculum, and other buildings now open or in development, students and faculty have begun writing their own chapter in Turkey's history.

Cannon Design

Texas Christian University Student Recreation Center
Fort Worth, Texas

The program for Texas Christian University's Student Recreation Center combines 104,000 square feet of new construction and 120,000 square feet of renovated space to create a unique campus attraction. The new addition includes an atrium lobby, three-court gymnasium, 12,000-square foot weight and fitness center, climbing wall, racquetball/squash courts, multipurpose room and mezzanine-level running track. The existing two-court gymnasium has been remodeled as an intercollegiate volleyball venue and recreation space, and the refurbished natatorium now offers a 25-yard, six-lane pool with diving well. Designed by Cannon Design in association with Hahnfeld Hoffer Stanford Architects, the new construction is clad in cream brick to harmonize with the existing structure. The curving metal roof over the weight and fitness center differentiates the award-winning building from its surroundings. In addition, extensive glazing lets sunlight flood and reveal the interior by day, and artificial illumination turns the building into a glowing beacon by night.

Upper left: Roof detail.

Upper right: Weight and fitness center.

Above: Atrium lobby.

Left: Night view.

Photography: Jon Miller/Hedrich Blessing.

Cannon Design

Florida Community College Advanced Technology Center
Jacksonville, Florida

Left: Entrance

Below: Classroom.

Bottom: Main elevation.

Photography: Neil Rashba.

Intended to evolve with the growing needs of manufacturers and high-tech employers in information technology, advanced manufacturing, biotechnology and transportation technology--all emerging fields targeted by the Jacksonville Economic Development Commission-Florida Community College's 115,000-square foot, three-story Advanced Technology Center in Jacksonville gives students an optimal environment for pre-service and in-service employee training. Housing laboratories, classrooms, administrative and faculty offices, and seminar and meeting rooms, the brick-clad Center is a new symbol for the rebirth of the College's urban campus. In honoring the project with a Merit Award for Excellence in Architecture, the American Institute of Architects jury stated, "The restraint of this building is appreciated, as well as the sophisticated use of brick, and excellent use of shadow." Not coincidentally, the Center also visibly affirms the College's mission to "being a leading partner in creating a dynamic, prosperous community of enlightened leaders and thoughtful, effective, global citizens."

Cannon Design

Suffolk University
Somerset Street Residence Hall
Boston, Massachusetts

Creating housing for 345 students, the 121,000-square foot, 19-story Somerset Street Residence Hall complements its historic Beacon Hill neighborhood in Boston and supports the University's evolution from a commuter school to a residential campus. The key organizing element of the building, one of the "greenest" in Boston, is a 19-story central atrium designed to harvest daylight and reduce heat loss and gain by buffering surrounding interior spaces. The atrium consists of transparent south and west-facing glass walls and skylights with interior surfaces of glass and aluminum. Devised to reflect and diffuse light to the ground floor and to bedrooms, lounges and common spaces on the floors above, the atrium simultaneously introduces a quality of daylight not found in the typical dormitory, and tempers the air to reduce heat gain and loss to dormitory rooms. The design also caters to the needs of its student residents with such amenities as a fitness/weight room, medical examination room, computer laboratory, cafeteria and laundry. At the dedication ceremony, University president David J. Sargent stated, "Students come to us from across the country and around the world, and we are proud to offer them a safe and pleasant environment in which they can fully realize the academic and cultural promise of their Beacon Hill surroundings."

Above right: Cafeteria.

Above: Interior atrium curtain wall detail.

Left: Somerset Street elevation.

Photography: Warren Patterson

Centerbrook

67 Main Street
Post Office Box 955
Centerbrook, CT 06409
860.767.0175
860.767.8719 (Fax)
www.centerbrook.com

Centerbrook

**Phillips Exeter Academy
Phelps Science Center
Exeter, New Hampshire**

Above: West facade and outdoor classroom with wetland teaching garden.

Top: East facade and campus context.

Above right: Lab interior with Harkness Table.

Opposite: Lobby curtainwall and whale skeleton.

Photography: Jeff Goldberg/ ESTO Photographics.

Twelve students and a teacher sitting around the "Harkness Table," a 7-foot x 11-foot oval table, to present and discuss their work in a participatory format provided the vision for the new, 81,500-square foot, four-story Phelps Science Center at Phillips Exeter Academy, the famed private preparatory school founded in 1781 in Exeter, New Hampshire. In fact, the entire facility, designed by Centerbrook Architects and Planners, reflects a rethinking of educational laboratory design, based on design workshops involving faculty, students, administration, trustees, local residents and officials. Consequently, the brick exterior respects the Academy's historic campus, while the interior is free to be bold and innovative. Science classrooms for each discipline surround a common laboratory where two or more classes can participate in experiments, accompanied by technician prep areas, faculty research laboratories, a scanning electron microscope room, 300-seat Grainger Auditorium, lounges, and a skylit auditorium lobby with central staircase. A touch of whimsy prevails in the lobby, a popular gathering and exhibit space. High above the terrazzo floor, the skeleton of a humpback whale recovered by teachers and students in Maine hovers like a protective spirit.

Centerbrook

National Outdoor Leadership School Headquarters
Lander, Wyoming

Above right: Rooftop garden.

Right: Exterior and courtyard.

Below: Courtyard landscape.

Opposite: Rooftop "leaf" canopy.

Photography: Jeff Goldberg/ESTO Photographics.

Perhaps relocating a headquarters from a town of 6,200 residents to a "more rural" site might seem compelling to one of the leading organizations for training people to be skilled outdoor leaders and educators. However, the National Outdoor Leadership School decided to leave the outlying areas untouched, and to keep contributing to the vitality of Lander, Wyoming.

The 51,500 square foot, three-story headquarters, designed by Centerbrook Architects and Planners, stands just one block north of the historic Noble Hotel, the School's student housing and symbolic center in Lander. The headquarters responds to both its surroundings and its occupants. Outside, three box-like volumes, finished in brick as are nearby structures, and stacked like hay bales form a square courtyard overseen by an iconic rooftop "leaf" canopy of unfinished steel. Inside, narrow floors and high ceilings maximize the use of natural light, which is shared by open offices on one side and alcoves for private offices and meeting areas on the other. For an organization founded in 1965 by Paul Petzoldt, a legendary mountaineer and now president emeritus, it's a facility over 75,000 graduates worldwide could call home.

Centerbrook

Quinnipiac University
Arnold Bernhard Library
Hamden, Connecticut

Having survived numerous transformations, from its founding in 1929 as Connecticut College of Commerce, a small business college in New Haven, to its current status as a private, co-educational institution for over 8,000 students in Hamden, Quinnipiac University is not afraid of change. Consider the recent renovation and expansion of Arnold Bernhard Library by Centerbrook Architects and Planners. Originally built in 1969, the 20,000 square foot Library underwent such major alterations as the remodeling of the front facade on the University Quadrangle to make its spire a beacon of light and to provide a stepped proscenium for socializing, concerts and ceremonies; the demolition and replacement of the rear with a 60,000 square foot addition; the reduction from three floors to two in the original building; and the integration of the new and original building with a central skylit rotunda surrounded by open balconies. Not only has the project enlarged the Library's physical capacity and updated its technological capability, it has used formal composition to express the validity of humanity's core philosophical concerns. On a campus where most of the buildings have been built since 1975, the Library convincingly justifies Quinnipiac's faith in architecture.

Left: Team study room.

Lower left: Central rotunda.

Bottom left: Tower and beacon on university quadrangle.

Lower right: Cyber cafe. Peter Aaron/ESTO Photographics.

Bottom right: Projecting bays in addition.

Opposite: Staircase in rotunda.

Photography: Jeff Goldberg/ ESTO Photographics. (except as noted)

Centerbrook

Yale University
Yale Child Study Center
New Haven, Connecticut

Above: Mark Simon's frog fountain in play court.

Left: Auditorium.

Far left: The Center as seen from Medical School courtyard.

Below: Harris Pavilion with auditorium porch overlooking play court.

Photography: Jeff Goldberg/ ESTO Photographics.

No matter how challenging the search for expansion space adjacent to their existing facilities was, the Yale Child Study Center was inspired by the need to care for children. The Center is a division of the Yale University School of Medicine and one of the world's leading institutions for the study of child development. Though the only open space imposed numerous restrictions, the recently completed renovation and expansion of the Center, designed by Centerbrook Architects and Planners, was thoughtfully guided by programming workshops involving Centerbrook and the Center's physicians, researchers, students and administrators. The project comprises the refurbishment of the existing ground floor entry, the Child Development Unit, and the construction of the new 22,000-square foot, six-story Neison and Irving Harris Pavilion. The brick-clad Pavilion works at an urban scale because it successfully unifies the odd geometries of neighboring buildings. Inside, clarity prevails as well because all floors but the second are arrayed with rings of offices around a central support area of administrative space, storage, bathrooms and kitchenettes. Offices are modular to allow for flexibility as research projects grow and shrink. On the seacond floor the auditorium is centrally located and is readily accessed from the main entry and from grade at the rear of the building. Here conferees can stroll to lunch in a nearby dining hall and look down from a porch to watch the Center's charges in the play court, doing what children everywhere enjoy doing.

Christner Inc.

7711 Bonhomme Avenue
St. Louis, Missouri 63105
314.725.2927
314.725.2928(Fax)
www.christnerinc.com

Christner Inc.

Westminster College
Wallace H. Coulter Science Center
Fulton, Missouri

Finding new ways to do old things has produced outstanding results for Westminster College, a private, coeducational college founded in 1851 that serves 800 undergraduates in Fulton, Missouri. To commemorate an historic visit by Winston Churchill in 1946, when he delivered his famous "Iron Curtain" speech, Westminster reconstructed the Church of St. Mary the Virgin, Aldermanbury, a 12th-century church redesigned by Sir Christopher Wren after the Great Fire of London, on its 86-acre campus. Now, the school is encouraging interdisciplinary collaboration in the natural sciences, mathematics, and information sciences through a new 40,000-square foot renovation and 40,000-square foot addition comprising the Wallace H. Coulter Science Center, designed by Christner Inc. The idea of joining an addition to the existing, U-shaped classroom building with a glass-roofed atrium as a central gathering place, encircled by three floors of laboratories, seminar rooms, faculty offices and lecture hall, emerged from conversations among architects, faculty, contractors, trustees and administration. The building is viewed as a recruitment springboard and step toward advancing the school's ranking in the sciences. Praising Christner, Dr. Fletcher Lamkin, Westminster's president, notes, "They listened to our needs and integrated the requests of our faculty into a superb building for science investigation and learning."

Above left: Exterior of addition.

Above right: Seminar room and atrium floor.

Below left: Main entrance linking old and new.

Bottom left: Laboratory.

Opposite: Atrium.

Photography: Sam Fentress.

Christner Inc.

Maryville University
Four Buildings
St. Louis, Missouri

Left: Art & Design Building detail.

Below: Studio and lobby.

Photography: Sam Fentress.

A student-centered learning environment, offering a satisfying life on campus as well as room for expanding academic and social activity, has been a goal for Maryville University since Christner developed a master plan for its sprawling, 130-acre St. Louis campus in 1995. The experience of the school, an independent, coeducational university founded in 1872 by the Religious of the Sacred Heart, shouldn't surprise other growing institutions: campuses must cultivate good connections between people and places. Maryville is making those connections by weaving a dense landscape of new buildings and courtyard spaces. Recently, the school advanced the master plan with four new buildings, designed by Christner, that include a 29,000-square foot University Center, 18,500-square foot Art & Design Building, 21,700-square foot Auditorium and 25,400-

Above: Lecture hall.

Right: Academic Center exterior.

Photography: Sam Fentress.

square foot Academic Center. As the campus hub, the University Center attracts commuter students and traditional students with a bookstore, snack bar, student offices, game room, quiet study lounge and meeting areas for study and informal activity. Dr. Keith Lovin, president of Maryville, reports, "I sense more energy on campus that invigorates the entire learning community."

Above: University Center front entrance.

Right, far right: Gathering space and quiet study lounge.

Photography: Sam Fentress.

Left: Proscenium stage and auditorium.

Above: University Center viewed from the quadrangle.

Photography: Sam Fentress.

Christner Inc.

The Center of Clayton
Clayton, Missouri

Above: Game room.

Right: Public entrance.

Below left and right: Competition pool and gymnasium.

Bottom right: Climbing wall.

Opposite: Main staircase.

Photography: Sam Fentress.

The folk wisdom that two can live as thriftily as one has a convincing showcase in a new, unique,124,000-square foot, two-level facility, The Center of Clayton, in Clayton, Missouri, designed by Christner. The Center is a facility any high school or community would love, incorporating gymnasiums, competition pool, leisure pool, jogging track, fitness facilities, climbing wall, meeting rooms and older adults center. In fact, The Center is available to both high school students in the School District of Clayton and residents of Clayton, a St. Louis suburb. The collaborative venture successfully bridges the realms of public education and public recreation by giving students a continuous walkway between Clayton High School and The Center while maintaining separate control and entry points for students and residents. Indoors, skylights, large windows and few walls reinforce the atmosphere that welcomes everyone to The Center.

Christner Inc.

Cardinal Ritter College Preparatory School
St. Louis, Missouri

Above: Chapel.

Right: Laboratory.

Below: Exterior.

Photography: Sam Fentress.

You can easily see how a good building improves the image of a community by walking though the Grand Center cultural district of St. Louis, where the new, 83,000-square foot, two-story home of Cardinal Ritter College Preparatory School, designed by Christner, has opened. Cardinal Ritter is an Archdiocesan high school founded in 1979 with its own independent board that represents the product of a unique partnership between the Archdiocese and the region's corporate, civic and philanthropic organizations—and occupies the City of St. Louis's first private high school built in 50 years. While the handsome, brick-clad structure anticipates future expansion on its 16.6-acre site by hugging the eastern edge at the terminus of Grandel Square, giving the building a commanding presence and room to grow, the inviting interior serves 400 students with classrooms, laboratories, commons, library, gymnasium and chapel. St. Louis's enthusiasm for Cardinal Ritter isn't based on faith alone, to be sure: nearly 100 percent of its students will attend college.

Drummey Rosane Anderson, Inc.

141 Herrick Road
Newton Center, MA 02459
617.964.1700
617.969.9054 (Fax)
www.DRAarchitects.com

Drummey Rosane Anderson, Inc.

Belchertown High School
Belchertown, Masssachusetts

Education is the shared responsibility of students, parents, educators and community in Belchertown, a Massachusetts community overlooking the Connecticut Valley. This profound commitment is not surprising, given the opening of the town's first public school in 1762, one year after its incorporation and 31 years after its founding. Education rewards Belchertown's population of 13,000 whether they have children or not, as is handsomely demonstrated by the recent opening of Belchertown High School, designed

by Drummey Rosane Anderson. The town considers the new, 175,000-square foot, three-story High School for 1,000 9th-12th grade students a civic building. The faculty, staff, administration and community leaders have planned the music, athletic, library/media and dramatic arts areas to serve the public during evenings and weekends,

supported by their own lobbies and the entrances. The resulting facility is user friendly despite multiple tasks. A "main street" corridor provides easy access by connecting strategically placed and well-equipped common areas for shared learning, including the gymnasium at one end and the auditorium and cafeteria at the other. Three lobbies are utilized, including a

main entrance/gymnasium lobby, a monumental, three-story staircase lobby rising to the library/media center, and a cafeteria/ auditorium lobby, to unify the space. Christine Parzych, principal of Belchertown High School, declares, "Our new building has given us the opportunity to provide our students with the very best educational experience."

Top right: Cafeteria/ auditorium lobby.

Upper right: Exterior.

Above: Library/media center.

Right: Auditorium.

Far right: Gymnasium.

Opposite: Cafeteria.

Photography: Greg Premru.

Drummey Rosane Anderson, Inc.
Peirce School
Arlington, Massachusetts

Increasing enrollments and the need for new technologies and flexible spaces ended the 75-year career of the original Peirce School in Arlington, Massachusetts, but the new Peirce School keeps more than its name alive by occupying the same, constrained site with significant slopes in a urban neighborhood. While the recently completed, 48,500-square foot, three-story building for 300 K-5 students, designed by Drummey Rosane Anderson, has a larger footprint than its predecessor, it covers much of the same ground to preserve existing playing fields. However, with its distinctive architecture, featuring curving forms that enclose the cafetorium, library, science room and art room and echo Arlington's many water towers, its interesting views from the major streets that surround the site, and its availability for community use, particularly the gymnasium, cafetorium and outdoor dining terrace, reached through a special, at-grade entry at the lower level, the Peirce School breaks new ground in an historic town, settled in 1635, where an early skirmish of the Revolutionary War was fought.

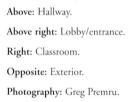

Above: Hallway.

Above right: Lobby/entrance.

Right: Classroom.

Opposite: Exterior.

Photography: Greg Premru.

Drummey Rosane Anderson, Inc.

Mildred Avenue Community Center Middle School
Mattapan, Massachusetts

Top right: Science laboratory.

Above left: Rear elevation.

Above right: Dance studio.

Right: Pool.

Below: Group learning space and lockers.

Opposite: Community center entrance.

Photography: Greg Premru.

As a true community school, the new, three-story Mildred Avenue Community Center Middle School in Mattapan, Massachusetts, designed by Drummey Rosane Anderson for 750 students, required an agreement between Boston Public Schools and Boston Community Centers to co-locate in one facility and share such program spaces as the pool, gymnasium, auditorium and cafeteria, plus operating costs. The results have been gratifying for everyone, in no small part due to the sensitive architectural handling of the ambitious building program on the restricted site in a residential neighborhood adjacent to commuter railroad tracks. The building's linear arrangement minimizes its footprint, reinforces the street line, respects the scale of adjacent "triple decker" houses. The arrangement-buffers such sensitive areas as the library, classrooms and offices from intermittent train noise with such components as the gymnasium, mechanical rooms, storage areas and kitchen. School and community comfortably share facilities while maintaining separate identities, security and operating hours. The masonry, aluminum and glass-clad structure's massing identifies the Community Center at the north end of the site as a distinct entity from the Middle School at the south end. Each institution's primary entrance has its own architectural vocabulary, lobby and direct visual supervision from adjacent administrative areas. The interior environment, features durable but colorful furnishings, ample daylight and indirect lighting, and a sophisticated HVAC system, puts both children and senior citizens at ease.

Drummey Rosane Anderson, Inc.

Duxbury Performing Arts Center
Duxbury, Massachusetts

Curtain up, Duxbury! On a campus occupied by the Massachusetts town's library, swimming pool, major playing fields, high school, middle school and an elementary school, the new, 40,000-square foot, two-story Duxbury Performing Arts Center represents both an obvious source of civic pride and an impressive example of theater design. Created by Drummey Rosane Anderson for multiple stage use by performers ranging from third graders to professionals, the Center houses a 1,100-seat theater, rehearsal space, green rooms, scene shop, band room, lobbies and dining facilities. Not only is it ready for school plays and musical programs, but the incorporation of such features as an orchestra pit, full fly with technical grid, and operable/adjustable proscenium opening with a caliper stage at each wing, facilitates major theater and musical stage productions. Yet the Center is also a good neighbor to adjacent buildings in a conservative community founded in 1628 by Captain Myles Standish and his fellow Pilgrims. The bulk of the performance hall's formidable mass is tempered by such smaller spaces as practice areas, dining hall, lobby and set construction that surround it. Of course, nothing is allowed to compromise the Center's performance. Susan Skeiber, principal of Duxbury's Alden School, happily observes, "The acoustics of the space are tremendous."

Above left: Rehearsal space.
Above right: Exterior.
Right: 1,100-seat theater.
Photography: Greg Premru.

104

Earl Swensson Associates, Inc.

2100 West End Avenue
Suite 1200
Nashville, Tennessee 37203
615.329.9445
615.329.0046 (Fax)
www.esarch.com

Earl Swensson Associates, Inc.

Earl Swensson Associates, Inc.

Belmont University
Beaman Student Life Center/Curb Event Center
Nashville, Tennessee

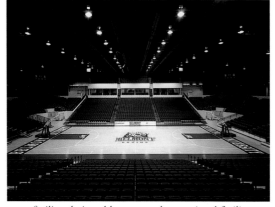

Above left: Exterior.

Above right: Café.

Right: Arena.

Far right: Climbing wall.

Opposite: Commons.

Photography: Scott McDonald/Hedrich Blessing, Kieran Reynolds Photography, Robt. Ames Cook.

Belmont University's 62-acre Nashville campus, featuring Belle Monte, the antebellum Italianate mansion of Joseph and Adelicia Acklen where the school was founded in 1890, has added another chapter to its history by opening the Beaman Student Life Center/Curb Event Center. Not only does the handsome, neoclassical-styled, 219,544-square foot, two-story facility, designed by Earl Swensson Associates with Cannon Design, consulting architect, consolidate athletic programs and student organizations previously scattered across the campus, it gives some 4,000 students a social gathering place everyone can enjoy. A 5,000-seat arena and multi-purpose sports and entertainment center, student fitness and recreational facility, office and meeting space for student services, grand concourse and Vince Gill Room (a special events space overlooking the arena), and atrium offer students numerous options. Not surprisingly, the Centers are active all day—including a 36-foot climbing wall.

Earl Swensson Associates, Inc.

Trevecca Nazarene University
Waggoner Library
Nashville, Tennessee

Above left: Circulation desk of curriculum collection.

Above right: Main entrance.

Left: Rotunda at night.

Far left: MBA lecture room.

Opposite: Interior of rotunda/reading room.

Photography: Robt. Ames Cook, Michael Lewis.

Libraries are anything but obsolete in the Internet era, as the new, 61,489-square foot, two-story (plus lower level) Waggoner Library at Nashville's Trevecca Nazarene University triumphantly demonstrates. The stately neoclassical structure, designed as a campus welcoming building by Earl Swensson Associates with such highlights as a colonnade/porch intended for social gatherings, and a rotunda, which serves as an identifiying beacon at night, makes information readily available in every format to the roughly 1,900 students attending the Christian-centered institution. Equally important, the stone-and-glass-clad structure provides a supportive environment for study and research. Everywhere students turn, from the lobby, grand reading room and stacks, MBA lecture room and rotunda, to the lower level's Center for Instructional Technology and advanced curriculum and media facilities, there are good lighting and acoustics, comfortable furnishings and Internet access. Why shouldn't a library be user friendly?

Earl Swensson Associates, Inc.

Ensworth Middle School
Nashville, Tennessee

Above: Commons room in Middle School.

Left: Library exterior.

Below: Lower school reading room.

Below left : Library discussion/reading area.

Opposite: Atrium in Middle School.

Photography: Gary Knight + Associates, Kieran Reynolds Photography

To see how intriguingly past and present can coexist in academia, consider the new Middle School and Library for The Ensworth School, a private, nonsectarian, coed school in Nashville founded in 1958. The two structures, encompassing 46,100 square feet, were designed by Earl Swensson Associates in the School's traditional Tudor style to extend campus construction beyond where the ground slopes to the athletic fields. On the outside, the Middle School academic building, whose three levels descend in step with the topography, and the Library, serving both the lower and middle schools, faithfully reflect the Tudor architecture that began with the site's original house, called Red Gables. Indoors, the two interiors offer state-of-the-art facilities. The Middle School's Patton Hall houses 15 classrooms, a computer laboratory and a commons room, dedicating one floor each with separate public spaces to the sixth, seventh and eighth grades. The interior of the Hortense Bigelow Ingram Library invites students to a modern resource center equipped with study rooms, a classroom, conference space and a discussion/reading area anchored by a monumental stone fireplace. As a final touch, the Library is connected by a common lobby to Red Gables, now housing Ensworth's administrative offices.

Earl Swensson Associates, Inc.

Battle Ground Academy Middle School
Franklin, Tennessee

Transmitting a shared, time-honored tradition to a new building while staking out a separate, contemporary identity through modern, cost-effective construction is a common challenge on school campuses that has been resolved with considerable skill at Battle Ground Academy, a college preparatory day school for 950 students in Franklin, Tennessee, founded in 1889. The school recently completed four one-story facilities enclosing 69,000 square feet for its Middle School, designed by Earl Swensson Associates. An administration and library building, academic building for grades 5, 6, 7 and 8, middle school athletic facility and fine arts academic building meant for the entire campus, all grouped around a motor court/plaza, pay homage to the shared high school campus's heritage of brick-and-stone construction, directly adopting such motifs as the colonnades, dormers, pre-cast medallions and pitched roofs. While one-story construction, incorporating wood-truss framing and simple geometrics, is consistent in buildings for both the middle and high school, distinct positioning and separate entries on the campus create the separate identities for the two schools.

Top left: Athletic facility.

Above left: Library.

Left: Motor court.

Photography: Robt. Ames Cook.

Elkus/Manfredi Architects

530 Atlantic Avenue
Boston, Massachusetts 02210
617.426.1300
617.426.7502 (Fax)
www.elkus-manfredi.com

Elkus/Manfredi Architects

Elkus/Manfredi Architects

Emerson College
Tufte Performance and Production Center
Boston, Massachusetts

The gateway to a city's theater district is not the usual place to search for a college campus, but that's where you'll find Boston's Emerson College, the nation's leading comprehensive college dedicated exclusively to communication and the arts in a liberal arts context. From its founding in 1880, Emerson has become a multi-faceted institution with an enrollment of 3,350 students that is recognized for excellence in such areas as communication, marketing, journalism, the performing arts, the visual and media arts, literary writing and publishing. Its ability to thrive within the tight quarters surrounding the theater district was recently tested during the development of its new, 76,000-square foot, 11-story (plus basement) Tufte Performance and Production Center, designed by Elkus/Manfredi Architects. To develop two double-height theater auditoriums (210-seat thrust stage, 130-seat end-stage), dressing rooms, make-up studio, costume studio, set design studio, two television studios and control rooms, classrooms, faculty offices and loading dock, as well as a dressing room and green room facilities for an adjacent performing arts venue, the Cutler Majestic Theater, the school and its architect arranged this unusual combination of complex, technical spaces to fit on its small, mid-block site through vertical stacking only with connections and access from adjacent buildings. Discussions with state building officials resolved questions about

Above left: End-stage theater auditorium.

Above right: Art gallery adjacent to end-stage theater.

Opposite: A sliver of kinetic light at the end of Allen's Alley provides a 21st century marquee for Emerson College.

Photography: Peter Vanderwarker, Benjamin Cheung.

Elkus/ Manfredi Architects

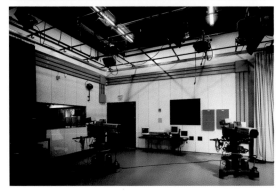

public access, fire separation, fire department access and emergency egress, enabling public access to be provided through an adjacent pedestrian alley and College-owned building. As a matter of fact, conventionality is rare in the award-winning design. The theater lobby for the thrust stage, for example, cantilevers over the service alley to provide necessary program area, and the entrance lobby is located beneath the alley to keep the ground floor open for service access to adjacent buildings. When the show must go on at Tufte Center, its handsome and versatile design ensures that it does.

Above left: Below-grade entry stairs to Tufte Center.

Above right: Views in descending order of dancing lights, control room and second television studio.

Left: View of service alley from cantilevered lobby.

Opposite: Exterior with illuminated stairwell.

Elkus/Manfredi Architects

Emerson College
Cutler Majestic Theater at Emerson College
Boston, Massachusetts

Left: Orchestra view of proscenium, where Ethel Barrymore, W. C. Fields, Al Jolson and Gloria Swanson once appeared.

Top: Stage view of orchestra and balconies, furnished with new seating that replicates original, plus wider aisles and more legroom.

Above: Exterior at Tremont Street and Allen's Alley.

Photography: Bruce T. Martin

More than a few proper Bostonians must have gazed in awe during the opening of the 1,200-seat Majestic Theater, designed by noted architect John Galen Howard, in 1903. Not only was the Majestic Boston's first theater without columns obscuring sight lines, thanks to cantilevered balconies spanning the inverted bowl-shaped auditorium, its telescoping arches were spectacularly illuminated by over 5,000 electric light bulbs, its acoustics were extraordinary, and its Beaux Arts design and decoration were superbly crafted in stone, wood, plaster, gold leaf and other uncompromising materials. Possibly the only thing more astonishing than the space itself is the fact that it remains an active, up-to-date performing arts hall today, thanks to an historic restoration and technological modernization of its entire 26,200-square foot, four-story structure by Emerson College with Elkus/Manfredi Architects. Its rebirth as the Cutler Majestic Theater at Emerson College not only safeguards the artistic integrity of the original theater, it gives the school an unparalleled showcase for its performing arts programs. However, the initial repairs that made the Majestic suitable for the performing arts in 1987 were just the first steps in undoing its conversion to a movie theater in 1956, which sealed off the second of two balconies, and decades of financial and physical decline. Under Elkus/

Elkus/Manfredi Architects

Left: Lobby, displaying original murals by William deLeftwich Dodge, has relocated ticket window for improved circulation.

Below left: Proscenium and telescoping arches, showing restored lighting design with 5,000 light bulbs.

Below right: Second balcony, hidden for nearly 50 years, now connects to lobby for first time.

Manfredi's care, the century-old landmark was restored to its original appearance as much as historic evidence allowed, accessibility and circulation issues were resolved in compliance with current building codes and ADA requirements, advanced building operating systems and theater equipment were installed, and back-stage facilities missing from the original design were provided in a new building Emerson was developing literally next door, the Tufte Performance and Production Center, also designed by Elkus/Manfredi. Is it fair to say the Cutler Majestic is as splendid as ever? In truth, it's probably better.

Goody Clancy

334 Boylston Street
Boston, MA 02116
617.262.2760
617.262.9512 (Fax)
www.goodyclancy.com

Goody Clancy

Purdue University Rawls Hall
Krannert Graduate School of Management
West Lafayette, Indiana

As proud as Purdue University is of historic strengths in engineering and agriculture, the West Lafayette, Indiana institution, founded in 1869 and named for benefactor John Purdue, has nurtured the Krannert Graduate School of Management into one of the nation's leading business schools. Krannert's ability to provide engineers and scientists with business skills was recently rewarded with an impressive, state-of-the-art teaching facility, Jerry S. Rawls Hall. This award-winning, 128,000 square-foot, four-story building, designed by Goody Clancy in association with Scholer Corporation, is named for the CEO of Finisar Corp., a Krannert graduate and leading donor to the building. In its well-equipped classrooms, breakout rooms, arena-style classrooms, 125-seat lecture hall, faculty and administration offices, four-story atrium, Student Forum, distance learning center, and laboratories for economics simulation as well as behavioral study and computers, students and faculty have an exceptionally inviting setting for study and interaction. Dean Richard Cosier has commented, "I think the building is so magnificent that it will give us an edge, all other things being equal."

Above: Exterior at night.

Below: Lecture hall.

Right: Atrium seating.

Opposite: Atrium.

Photography: Jon Denker/ Commercial Architectural Photography Services. Barbara Karaut

Goody Clancy

North Kingstown High School
North Kingstown, Rhode Island

North Kingstown has every reason to feel special as "Rhode Island's Sea Town." This historic community of some 24,000 residents, founded as part of the original Kings Towne in 1674, is blessed with a natural harbor, beaches and resort accommodations. Additionaly, revered sites such as Smith's Castle (1678), the site of trading centers established by Richard Smith and RogerWilliams; Old Narragansett Church (1707), the oldest Episcopal Church building north of Philadelphia; Casey Farm (mid-18th century), one of New England's oldest working farms; and Wickford Village, one of America's finest assemblages of houses from the late 18th and early 19th centuries. Now,

with the opening of the handsome, 250,000-square foot, three-story North Kingstown High School, designed by Goody Clancy, in association with Saccoccio Associates, on grounds that encompass a 2,000-seat stadium, playing fields, tennis court and outdoor teaching areas, the town can record another chapter in its history by taking advantage of an educational environment intended to be used jointly by the school and the community. The brick-clad building's state-of-the-art classrooms, library, 800-seat auditorium, gymnasium, 600-seat cafeteria, administrative offices, reception, and specialized facilities for art, music and industrial arts are organized around a sun-filled, three-story "main street" atrium. This

links the civic, front-entry plaza, an informal, sun-filled "village green" courtyard, and academic wing. As a gathering place for students, faculty and residents, the atrium should give North Kingstown a lively forum to shape its fourth century.

Top left: Front entry.

Top right: West entry.

Above: Library.

Opposite: "Main Street" atrium.

Photography: Richard Mandelkorn.

Goody Clancy

Bentley College Student Center
Waltham, Massachusetts

Can a strategically located student center improve the quality of life on a 163-acre college campus in Waltham, Massachusetts, for some 5,600 full-time and part-time undergraduate and graduate students? For Bentley College, a business university founded in 1917 that provides housing for 80 percent of its full-time undergraduates, the development of the new, 70,000-square foot, three-story Student Center, designed by Goody Clancy, has given everyone an appealing opportunity to pause on a path between the classrooms and the dormitories. The steel and wood-framed structure, which is finished in brick under a metal and slate roof, encloses a 500-seat dining hall with kitchen and servery, 100-seat private dining room/pub, game rooms, multi-purpose rooms, living room with fireplace,

offices and workspaces for student organizations, chapel, conference rooms, lounges and social gathering spaces. Friendly, informal, comfortable and ruggedly built, the award-winning design nestles on a wooded slope with entry points on two levels at opposite ends, and has become a magnet to students no matter where "home" is.

Left: Entrance.

Below left: Exterior.

Below right: Servery.

Opposite: Dining hall.

Photography: Warren Jagger.

Goody Clancy

Massachusetts Institute of Technology
Dreyfus Chemistry Laboratories
Cambridge, Massachusetts

Because three decades had visibly aged the Dreyfus Chemistry Laboratories at Massachusetts Institute of Technology in Cambridge, remedial action on its 130,000-square foot, seven-story structure, originally designed by I.M. Pei & Partners, was unavoidable. However, the challenge to Goody Clancy had a twist. The architect would improve outdated research spaces that isolated researchers, expand natural lighting, increase fume hoods by 40 percent without losing any research area or occupant count, improve access, flexibility and overall quality and safety within the environment, replace every mechanical, electrical, plumbing, laboratory service and life system, and restore the exterior envelope to improve energy efficiency and prevent water penetration. But the three-year restoration and renovation would proceed while the building remained mostly occupied, and ongoing research had to continue. Consequently, the design team developed a multi-phase construction process to keep two-thirds of the space operating at all times, inspiring individuals like chemistry professor Richard Danheiser to exclaim, "The contrast between the old and new labs is incredible!"

Above left: Light filled corridors & research areas.

Above right: Restored exterior.

Right: Laboratories.

Photography: Anton Grassl, Jerry Shereda, Andy Ryan.

Grimm + Parker Architects

2 Bethesda Metro Center
Suite 1350
Bethesda, MD 20814
240.223.0500
240.223.0510 (Fax)

11785 Beltsville Drive
Suite 1400
Calverton, MD 20705
301.595.1000
301.595.0089 (Fax)

1355 Beverly Road
Suite 105
McLean, VA 22101
703.903.9100
703.903.9755 (Fax)
www.grimmandparker.com

Grimm + Parker Architects

Queen Anne's High School
Centreville, Maryland

Above: Main entrance.

Left: Auditorium & Main St. Axis.

Right: Lobby.

Opposite: Lobby tower.

Photography: Kenneth Wyner.

As the older of two high schools in Queen Anne's County, on Maryland's Eastern Shore, Queen Anne's High School has responded to the arrival of a newer high school in a creative and satisfying way. A recent modernization and addition, designed by Grimm + Parker Architects, has dramatically transformed the once nondescript, technology-based school, which opened in 1966, into a dynamic, 221,067-square foot, two-story, 21st-century environment with a strong sense of identity and belonging. The award-winning design focuses on Queen Anne's existing and easily understood circulation system, which now features a Main Street for core circulation. Illuminated by a clerestory and windows that bring in daylight and views, Main Street extends through the building to connect such vital facilities as the auditorium, attendance/administration, guidance/careers, dining, student government, school store, art rooms and gymnasium, making it a valued gathering place for students, faculty and community alike.

Grimm + Parker Architects

Loyola Blakefield
Knott Hall
Baltimore, Maryland

How do you construct a new student commons around a school's existing gymnasium, replace an existing pool, enlarge locker rooms, reorient the school's main entry and create a new central quadrangle, all without disrupting everyday activities? The solution for Loyola Blakefield, a Catholic boys' school in Baltimore founded in 1852 by the Society of Jesus for grades 6-12, was to work with Grimm + Parker Architects on a phased construction project spanning three years to develop Knott Hall, a 130,000-square foot, three-story, Collegiate Gothic-style building. The latest addition to Loyola Blakefield's scenic, 65-acre campus has quickly assumed its role as the center of campus life.

Besides housing such new and upgraded athletic facilities as an aquatic center, locker and training rooms, coaching offices, wrestling and fitness centers and field house, Knott Hall introduces a new student commons featuring a dining hall, student and alumni lounges, hall of alumni, conference and class room facilities, bookstore and offices for Christian service, campus ministry, admissions, athletics and the Assistant Headmaster for Students. Loyola Blakefield's mission to educate young men who are "Intellectually Competent, Open to Growth, Religious, Loving and Committed to Justice and Integrity" has a new and inspiring symbol.

Above: Dining room.

Above left: Main entry.

Left: Arcade to Athletic Facilities

Photography: Ken Wyner

Grimm + Parker Architects

Frostburg Library
Frostburg, Maryland

Below: Children's area.

Above right: Street facade.

Below Right: Circulation desk.

Photography: Dan Cunningham.

Frostburg is a picturesque, historic community in western Maryland founded in 1811 whose resiliency in the face of major economic changes has secured the well-being of its residents, who currently number approximately 8,075 year-round residents and 5,400 full-time students at Frostburg State University. In fact, the recent completion of the new, 20,000-square foot Frostburg Library, designed by Grimm + Parker Architects, typifies the city's pragmatic approach to new ideas. Though the need for a larger, better-equipped library to replace a rapidly deteriorating one had been evident for years, Frostburg faced a number of unresolved issues,

including the challenging grade conditions at the downtown site, the loss of the site's parking spaces, and the need for state and local funding. Frostburg officials formed a close collaboration with the architects to resolve these issues, resulting in a one-story library sitting atop a one-story parking structure, and a cost-effective, award-winning library design described in documents prepared by Grimm + Parker to help secure funding. Compact as the library is, it provides a public meeting room, children's area, young adult area, adult area, fiction/non-fiction, periodicals, computers, children's program room and staff meeting rooms, and such amenities as skylights, restrooms and a

reading lounge in the building's tower. Frostburg's mayor, John Bambacus, proudly declares, "It is truly an enhancement to our Main Street, and will be a landmark for our community."

Grimm + Parker Architects

Myrtilla Miner Elementary School
Washington, D.C.

Top left: Extended learning area.

Above left: Media center.

Above right: Main elevation and entrance.

Photography: Kenneth Wyner.

When the District of Columbia Public Schools told Grimm + Parker Architects to design a new, 85,000-square foot, two-story replacement building for Myrtilla Miner Elementary School quickly, it set a 20-month schedule for design and construction. However, that didn't mean short-changing the 525 students of an institution founded in 1962 to honor Miner (1815-1864), a pioneering black educator. To develop a quality facility including classrooms, cafetorium, administration, media center, large group instruction, and science and computer laboratories, the architects modified a prototype plan to satisfy specific program requirements and acknowledge the surrounding neighborhood. The new, award-winning school rose swiftly behind the existing one. Despite its rapid development, Myrtilla Miner offers a supportive environment where public spaces are zoned along a main axis, academic wings form a loop organized around a media center, and such details as ceramic tile accents, carpeted areas, sophisticated lighting and a visual theme based on the four seasons help promote Myrtilla Miner's goal of quality education for African Americans.

Grimm + Parker Architects

Connelly School of the Holy Child
Potomac, Maryland

The educational philosophy of Cornelia Connelly (1809-1879) is based on individualized, compassionate education in which teacher and parents lead pupils by love rather than by fear, teacher and parent trust and support each student to develop her own style, and teacher and parent provide time for recreation and a stimulating variety of learning experiences. It's a philosophy that clearly thrives at the new, 33,429-square foot, three-story Library and Middle School for the Connelly School of the Holy Child, in Potomac, Maryland. The award-winning design, by Grimm + Parker Architects, makes efficient use of an extremely tight site to establish a new campus character and identity for the Catholic, independent, college preparatory middle and upper school for 465 young women, grades 6 through 12, founded in 1961. Organized on an H-shaped plan, the school places the library and hearth at its center, with art, music, computer laboratories and library on the first floor, classrooms on the second floor, and science laboratories and locker commons on the basement level. While the building's technology is advanced, its architecture of stone, brick, concrete and steel, with interiors of wood wainscoting, carpet, slate and VCT floors, and warm lighting, reaffirm timeless values. Commenting on the efforts of Grimm + Parker, principal Maureen Appel says, "On behalf of the entire Holy Child community, thank you for making our school a success."

Above left: Exterior elevation.

Above right: Library and hearth.

Left: Gallery/central stair.

Photography: Kenneth Wyner.

Grimm + Parker Architects

Matapeake Elementary School
Stevensville, Maryland

Matapeake Elementary School, the newest of eight elementary schools in Maryland's Queen Anne's County, uses basic, industrial metal construction to extraordinary effect by celebrating its unique ecological location on Kent Island in the Chesapeake Bay. Embracing a nautical theme as its design motif, the 68,221-square foot, one-story structure of corrugated metal wall panels and exposed structural steel framing, designed by Grimm + Parker Architects, orients its interior spaces to a linear, naturally illuminated Promenade and a central outdoor environmental Courtyard. The arrangement enables Matapeake's approximately 600 students in pre-kindergarten through fifth grade to use both indoor spaces and "outdoor rooms" for learning, encouraging students and faculty to interact, and fostering a strong sense of identity. Not only does the design transcend its modest budget to give students and faculty a full complement of classrooms, media center, dining hall and kitchen, gymnasium with stage and amphitheater, administration, student support services and building support services. Matapeake creates ongoing opportunities for learning that actually involve the world directly outside its classrooms, a situation rarely encountered even in schools that cost far more.

Above left: Main entrance with canopy.

Above right: Media center.

Left: Naturally illuminated Promenade.

Below left: Environmental courtyard.

Photography: Kenneth Wyner.

HMC Architects

3270 Inland Empire Blvd.
Ontario, CA 91764
800.350.9979
909.483.1400 (Fax)
www.hmcarchitects.com

HMC Architects

HMC Architects

Fontana High School
Steeler Hall
Fontana, California

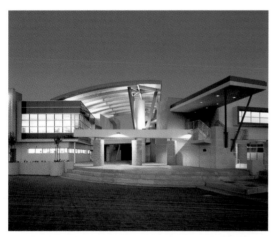

With 4,200 students projected for next year, Fontana High School, Fontana, California, is likely to become the Golden State's 15th largest high school. It is the largest high school in the Fontana Unified School District, serving Southern California's fast-growing Inland Empire, 50 miles east of Los Angeles. The completion of the dynamic, 48,000-square foot, two-story Steeler Hall, designed by HMC Architects, alleviates overcrowding by introducing new facilities for science and business as well as addressing standing master plan issues on the school campus. Consequently, there is space for class-rooms, laboratories, food service, student services, student store, student government and administration in the structure. The two wings radiating from the student center complement the existing modern architecture, and create a student-centered focus on the campus. Tom Reasin, principal of Fontana High School, proudly observes, "This is one project in particular that shows the district cares about the students and our school."

Top: Approach to Steeler Hall.

Upper left: Student center.

Lower left: Science wing.

Right: Entry courtyard.

Photography: Fred Daly.

HMC Architects

Azusa Pacific University
Duke Academic Complex
Azusa, California

Left: Principal elevation.

Below left: Art display panels.

Below right: Skylight.

Opposite: Entry facade.

Photography: Foaad Farah.

A high-bay tilt-up industrial warehouse in Azusa, California, would hardly seem like a candidate for conversion to a spacious, light-filled and inviting academic center. However, the impressive, new, 60,000-square foot (phase one of three), two-story Duke Academic Complex for Azusa Pacific University, designed by HMC Architects, convincingly transcends its past as it prepares to house the University's Schools of Theology, Art and Nursing, as well as the University Art Gallery. By removing a substantial portion of the warehouse for a courtyard, the renovation has reduced its footprint and number of firewalls required due to its connection to other University structures. The resulting composition should prove both versatile and attractive to the nearly 6,000 students of this evangelical Christian university, founded in 1899. For example, the courtyard features a fountain, landscaping and sculpture garden, with a snack bar and outdoor seating planned for future installation. Daylight floods the interior through a concrete, metal and glass entry facade, large windows in the firewalls and two-story lightwells. Making a virtue of its industrial origin, the interior embraces a high-tech look by exposing its steel and wood structure and adding materials such as a wire mesh ceiling grid, perforated metal art display panels and cast-in-place concrete, simultaneously acknowledging its past and welcoming its future.

HMC Architects

Lewis Elementary School
Yermo, California

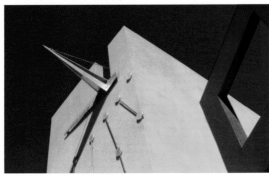

You would have to combine Rhode Island and Delaware to match the 3,200-square mile area served by the Silver Valley Unified School District. The district opened the 55,000-square foot, one-story Lewis Elementary School, in Yermo, California, designed by HMC Architects. Located in the high desert of Southern California between Los Angeles and Las Vegas, the district serves the communities of Calico, Daggett, Fort Irwin, Ludlow and Newberry Springs as well as Yermo with two elementary schools, one elementary/middle school, one middle school, one high school and an alternative education site. It's easy to see how Lewis Elementary School draws inspiration from its desert setting for the forms, massing and color of its award-winning architecture and interior design. Bringing a sense of wonder about the desert to the school is consistent with the district's belief that education should be housed in an animated environment that stimulates the senses, is fun to experience and reaffirms the joy of life. Thus, the classrooms, kindergarten, library, kitchen, cafetorium and administrative offices are all grouped around an outdoor learning courtyard. The architecture embraces the school's 762 K-3 students in expansive spaces, saturated colors and plentiful daylight supplemented by subtle electric illumination. For families in the rapidly growing Riverside-San Bernardino metropolitan region, Lewis Elementary School offers a splendid place for children to begin studying the world around them.

Above left: Cafetorium.

Top right: Library.

Above right: Principal's office.

Right: Sundial on tower.

Opposite above: Kindergarten entrance.

Opposite below: Outdoor learning courtyard.

Photography: Courtesy HMC Architects.

HMC Architects

University of California, San Diego
The Preuss School
La Jolla, California

Though too many young people never realize their potential as adults, disadvantaged students attending the Preuss School at University of California, San Diego, in La Jolla, receive an academically rigorous pre-collegiate education that gives them the opportunity they deserve. Now, thanks to an exceptional new, 72,000-square foot, two-story building, designed by HMC Architects, the

Preuss School has equipped its outstanding facility with a physical plant that actively supports them in helping up to 700 middle school and high school students. The award-winning facility, which includes classrooms, learning resource center/library, food service and administration, incorporates advanced technologies networked to the UCSD campus. In addition, there are such amenities as an

outdoor amphitheater that seats the entire student body, spacious and versatile classroom wings, a modern science wing for all grade levels, and a multipurpose room/performance area that can be teamed with the amphitheater for school and community events. The school's hope of creating a model for the nation shines brighter than ever.

Above: Campus entrance.

Right: Amphitheater.

Far right: Classroom.

Photography: HMC.

Mackey Mitchell Associates

800 St. Louis Union Station
The Power House
St. Louis, MO 63103-2257
314.421.1815
314.421.5206 (Fax)
www.mackeymitchell.com

Mackey Mitchell Associates

Washington University
The Village
St. Louis, Missouri

Founded in 1853, Washington University in St. Louis enjoys worldwide esteem as an independent research university whose 6,509 undergraduates and 5,579 graduate and professional students consistently give it high marks in national surveys on student satisfaction. The school's commitment to excellence has been impressively reaffirmed with the completion of the 148,500 GSF, four-story, 400-bed residential complex known as The Village, located on the north side of the 169-acre Hilltop Campus. This cluster of four buildings enclosing a quadrangle has been meticulously designed in Collegiate Gothic style to reinforce the prevailing campus architecture, which includes a number of buildings on the National Register of Historic Places. Acknowledging the importance of fraternities and sororities in campus life, the two smaller buildings adopt a town-house-type configuration for "Greek" use, while the two larger buildings follow a conventional horizontal dormitory layout with single semi-suites. The Village enjoys a degree of self-sufficiency by incorporating a food service on the ground level and such student support services as a black-box theater, music practice rooms, classrooms and seminar/study rooms on the lower level of the building on the south side of the quadrangle. It's even designed to take on an entirely new mission, exchanging bedrooms for classrooms or other academic functions, if that's what Washington University needs in its second century and beyond.

Left: Coffered ceiling in stairwell.

Lower left: Living room.

Lower right: Staircase seating nook.

Opposite: Northwest corner.

Photography: Sam Fentress.

Mackey Mitchell Associates

St. Louis College of Pharmacy
Dining Hall, Residential Tower, and Teaching Labs
St. Louis, Missouri

Call it the Cinderella effect if you will, but the tired, gritty, five-acre campus of St. Louis College of Pharmacy, an independent, non-sectarian college founded in 1864, has emerged resplendent from the renovation of the main academic building and the construction of a new residential tower and dining hall in the heart of St. Louis' Central West End Medical Community. The project has decisively transformed the College's image. The new residential tower, for example, took the place of a parking lot, letting the existing residence hall yield to a new, central quadrangle. The new dining hall was

then located beside the new campus green as soon as Parkview, an existing street that bisected the campus, was converted into a pedestrian mall, creating a people-friendly environment. As a vertical solution to a limited site, the 300-bed residential tower gives most students double semi-suites while upperclassmen receive single suites on the top floors. Simultaneously, the 288-seat dining hall, a light, airy pavilion offering views of the quadrangle by day and casting a warm glow on the campus by night, has become the favorite place for academic and social events—as well as a good meal. Teaching labs were designed to be

multi-functional spaces. Concepts can be explained through any method available in the classroom set-ups, and immediately applied. Labs are fully wired, along both laptop and benchtop learning. Pharmacy labs simulate the workplace environment for compounding and dispensing drugs, as well as for patient examination and counseling. In all labs, safety is a prime consideration; benches are arranged to allow the instructors to see each student's work and have quick access to them.

Above: Dining hall at night, with residential tower to its left and Lab building on right.

Left: Dining room.

Photography: Alise O'Brien

Mackey Mitchell Associates

Saint Louis University
Busch Student Center
St. Louis, Missouri

Saint Louis University, founded in 1818, is one of America's top research institutions. It also happens to be the oldest university west of the Mississippi, and the second oldest Jesuit Catholic university in the United States. It was time for the 35-year-old Busch Student Center to become a contemporary destination site on its Frost campus in St. Louis, providing "pizzazz" as well as additional space to hold events. Now that the renovation and expansion of the 160,000-square foot facility are finished, the design is exceeding expectations. An ambitious program to update exterior and interior finishes, enhance adjacent public areas and create green space, turn dining rooms into destinations and social centers for student entertainment and relaxation, and construct 42,000 square feet of new banquet and meeting facilities for up to 1,600 people has resulted in new vitality at the center. Its prominent location on Grand Avenue, a major east-west traffic artery in midtown St. Louis is home to Grand Center, the city's leading cultural district. Better yet, over 7,000 undergraduates and 4,000 graduate students are discovering the new bookstore, coffee shop, fast-food outlets, recreation venues and numerous other reasons to keep returning.

Above: Main entry.

Left: Pre-function corridor for ballrooms.

Photography: Sam Fentress.

149

Mackey Mitchell Associates

Washington University
Student Housing and Ursa's Café
St. Louis, Missouri

Top: Clock tower plaza.

Above left: Ursa's Café.

Above right: Village spine.

Left: Plug-and-play tables at Ursa's Café.

Photography: James Leick (Top), Barclay Goeppner (Ursa's Cafe), Alise O'Brien (Village Spine).

An interesting development is changing the residential system at Washington University in St. Louis by inaugurating a series of residential colleges in the spirit of Great Britain's legendary Oxford and Cambridge universities. Not only does each college house 150 freshmen and 150 upperclassmen in facilities with program spaces to support its mission, it maintains its own outdoor space and individual identity. A focus of this effort can be found on the South Forty campus, where Mackey Mitchell Associates is implementing a housing master plan it developed in 1995 for 3,000 beds. South Forty's unique hierarchy of outdoor spaces helps reinforce a sense of community, employing a "green" for public recreation and events, a "village spine" of outdoor social spaces and retailing that functions as a main street to the main campus, and a "clock tower plaza" that acts as the social hub. To offer students on-campus recreation, there is Ursa's Café, an inviting, 7,250 square foot space facing "clock tower plaza," where students can enjoy conviviality, quiet contemplation, poetry readings or live music with their food and beverage in comfort and style.

Mackey Mitchell Associates

Central Institute for the Deaf
St. Louis, Missouri

Below: Main entrance.

Bottom: Boardroom.

Photography: Sam Fentress.

Hearing impaired children and young adults have turned to the Central Institute for the Deaf in St. Louis since 1914, the year Dr. Max Aaron Goldstein established it to help them listen, speak and succeed in the mainstream. Now, an inviting and caring "village" is opening new possibilities for the Institute at the Highway 40 entrance to Washington University Medical Center in St. Louis, following a three-phase renovation and expansion program. Phases I and II, covering two new buildings of 42,000 square feet and 65,000 square feet designed in the existing Italianate style, and Phase III, renovating a 1928 building of 31,000 square feet, have endowed the Institute with state-of-the-art research and teaching facilities and the latest technologies. Shared spaces for academic and social events are revitalizing Dr. Goldstein's legacy.

Mackey Mitchell Associates

University of Cincinnati
Stratford Heights Student Housing
Cincinnati, Ohio

Top: View from the main campus.

Above: Student Center.

Illustration: Paul Wunnenberg, AIA Mackey Mitchell Associates.

Can collegiate fraternities and sororities live harmoniously in a community designed for sharing resources and fostering cooperation? That's the inspiration behind Stratford Heights at the University of Cincinnati, an innovative, new, 10.4 acre development. It was designed by Mackey Mitchell Associates to house 696 students in 14 buildings with 500 parking spaces in Cincinnati's University Heights neighborhood, just west of the main campus. The "Greek" village surrounds a central lawn and pedestrian mews that students will take to and from the main campus when they are not using it for recreation. Each building, designed in the English Tudor style and generously landscaped to blend into the existing neighbor-hood of single-family and duplex homes, will typically house one organization with its own entry, front porch, living room, activity rooms, and double semi-suites. A versatile student center will also encourage interaction among "Greeks" by offering a delicatessen, convenience store, fitness center, party room, pub room and computer laboratory where they can assemble for socializing, relaxation and quiet study. As a new venture for an associated institution founded in 1819 and justly proud of such historic "firsts" as oral polio vaccine, safe anti-knock gasoline and antihistamine, Stratford Heights seems to have the right stuff.

Mithun

Pier 56, 1201 Alaskan Way
Suite 200
Seattle, WA 98101
206.623.3344
206.623.7005 (Fax)
www.mithun.com

Mithun

University of Washington
Nordheim Court
Seattle, Washington

Left: Stoops at street edge.

Right: "Antenna Reeds" sculpture.

Below left: Neighborhood courtyard.

Below right: Townhouse with operable windows.

Opposite: Stair to plaza

Photography: Doug Scott Photography

Student housing which is too good to be student housing is one way to describe the new, award-winning and highly popular Nordheim Court at the University of Washington in Seattle. Eight three- to five-story buildings are organized into neighborhoods around an interior street, plaza and pond, totaling 176,000 square feet, 146 units of housing for 460 students near Seattle's University Village

neighborhood. What a casual visitor might overlook is the care that made the development a marketing success among freshman and sophomore students, as well as a triumph for cost effective environmental design. Working closely with students, neighbors and the University, Mithun created a concept to provide stimulating indoor and outdoor spaces, and promote a sustainable environment. Consequently,

the project offers a variety of housing units, ranging from standard furnished apartments to four-bed-room townhouses, along with a community center, exercise room, mail facility and laundry. Landscape amenities were integrated throughout to provide recreational opportunities, help conceal a 150-car underground parking garage and provide stormwater retention. Equally important has been the adoption of sus-

tainable design principles using the USGBC's LEED™ criteria to identify alternatives to conventional materials, and methods to lower the developer /property manager's initial and long-term costs which will result in LEED™ Certified Rating for the project. The success of Nordheim Court could inspire similar efforts across the nation.

Mithun

Portland State University
Stephen Epler Hall
Portland, Oregon

It's easy to imagine Stephen Epler Hall, Portland State University's new 64,000 square foot, six-story, 130-unit student housing facility, winning the approval of the man it honors, the late Dr. Stephen E. Epler. A principled, persistent and resourceful educator, Dr. Epler founded the school in 1946 as an extension of the Oregon Board of Higher Education, and steered it safely past its opponents to create Oregon's largest university, which now serves 22,000 students on its 45-acre campus. Besides housing 156 students, this "live/learn" facility provides classrooms, academic offices and community space. The award-winning design by Mithun embraces sustainable principles and is on track to be the University's first USGBC LEED™ Certified building. What makes the design so impressive is its extensive use of environmentally sound materials and methods, which extend to the daily operation of the building in ways visible to all. The courtyard, for example, creates a cool microclimate for the natural ventilation for 97 percent of the building, an idea Dr. Epler would have appreciated.

Top right: West façade at street level.

Above left: Northwest corner of exterior.

Above right: Courtyard at twilight.

Left: West façade with sun-screens and shade trees.

Opposite: "Splash box" to capture rain water.

Photography: Eckert & Eckert

Mithun

IslandWood
Bainbridge Island, Washington

Building sites occupy just six out of 255 acres at IslandWood, a residential environmental education campus for children and adults 14 miles west of Seattle, Washington. Founded by Paul and Debbi Brainerd in 2002, a curriculum of science, technology and the arts was developed through a community-wide effort engaging children, scientists, teachers, artists, historians, and interested citizens. The subsequent program called for educational structures, extensive trail systems and outdoor field structures to meet the client's mission of experiential-based learning. Each year, 4,000 fourth and fifth graders arrive to spend three days and nights exploring IslandWood. Mithun

and the landscape architects, The Berger Partnership, intended the campus to serve as a model of environmentally sound design principles. The IslandWood site encompasses a nearly complete watershed including numerous wetlands, a bog, a pond, a stream, and different examples of native northwest landscapes. The site has been logged extensively for the past 130 years, and an overlay mapping exercise comparing logging history, steep slopes, soil suitability and wetland areas was used to locate the least fragile building sites for the 40 buildings and site structures. The buildings themselves demonstrate how sustainable design can improve everything from site selection and

Above left: Dining Hall interior.

Left: Dining Hall exterior.

Below left: Friendship Circle open-air structure.

Below right: Welcome Center interior.

Opposite: Art Studio exterior.

Mithun

material specifications to furnishings, operations and maintenance, to productivity and indoor air quality. Placing structures such as the Dining Hall, Learning Studio, Welcome Center, Lodges, Art Studio and graduate student and staff housing on the north edge of solar meadows allow for maximum solar access and offer framed views of the forest beyond. Materials were chosen to minimize their impact and need for finishes, leaving steel and wood building components exposed and unfinished, and using salvaged materials. In the same spirit, sustainable design ideas have enabled the buildings to substitute natural ventilation for air conditioning, capture and modify daylighting, reduce water usage with composting toilets and rainwater collection, and treat all building wastewater on-site through a blackwater treatment system. Do

accomplishments like these merit a USGBC LEED™ Gold Rating? They should and they have.

Right: Geological "vertical textbook" fireplace in one of three Lodges.

Lower left: Wetland Laboratory.

Lower right: Learning Studios exterior elevation.

Photography: Doug Scott Photography, Roger Williams, Art Grice.

Sasaki Associates, Inc.

64 Pleasant Street
Watertown MA 02472
617.926 3300
617.924.2748 (Fax)
www.sasaki.com

Sasaki Associates, Inc.

Johns Hopkins University
Ralph S. O'Connor Recreation Center
Baltimore, Maryland

How important are sports and physical fitness at the nation's most prestigious institutions? Ralph S. O'Connor, a 1951 graduate of Johns Hopkins University, has shared his passion for athletic activity with his illustrious, Baltimore-based alma mater by giving generously toward the construction of the new building that bears his name, the 63,000-square foot, four-level Ralph S. O'Connor Recreation Center. The modern, brick-clad structure, designed by Sasaki Associates, abuts the Newton H. White Jr.

Athletic Center, a varsity sports facility built in 1964 on the 128-year-old University's Homewood campus. Designed for students, faculty and staff, the O'Connor Recreation Center caters to non-athletes as well as varsity stars by offering such varied facilities as a weight room, fitness center, 30-foot climbing wall, racquetball/squash courts, jogging track, and a 18,000-square foot gymnasium that can be set up as three basketball courts, five volleyball courts or three badminton courts. Also included are adminis-

trative and coaches' offices, locker rooms, a lobby and waiting area, classrooms, multi-purpose rooms, support space and storage. It has fit into campus life so quickly that University project manager Frances Hammer insists, "It feels like it was here all along and yet is quite a contemporary building."

Top right: Fitness center.

Upper right: Internal stairway.

Right: Exterior as seen from Athletic Center.

Opposite: Main entrance.

Photography: Greg Hursley.

Sasaki Associates, Inc.

University of Balamand
Master Plan
Koura Valley, Lebanon

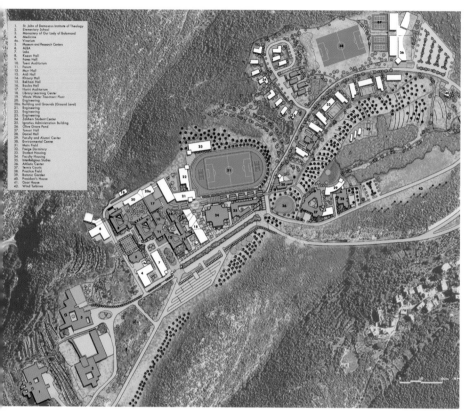

Above left: Site plan.

Above right: Engineering Courtyard.

Right: Student residences.

Below: Outdoor amphitheater.

Illustration:
Sasaki Associates, Inc.

In the aftermath of the Lebanese civil war, His Beatitude Patriarch Ignatius IV, Patriarch of the Antiochian Orthodox Christian Church, established the University of Balamand in 1988 as a private, non-profit, independent institution. It is dedicated to the promotion of better Christian-Moslem understanding as well as the study of the arts, humanities, sciences and professional fields that serve the needs of the regional community. Because the University intends to expand rapidly over the next 20 years, raising its current enrollment of over 1,800 students to 5,000, it retained Sasaki Associates to develop a master plan for its spectacular, 330,000-square meter hillside site in Lebanon's Koura Valley. Here olive and oak trees, wild flowers, mountain herbs and distinctive rock formations overlook the Mediterranean

Sea and the City of Tripoli. The master plan organizes the campus along a Path of Learning that links the secular realm, expressed by an ancient, stone-vaulted goat house restored as a faculty center at the upper end of the campus, to the spiritual realm, symbolized by the historic 12th century Abbey of Balamand at the lower end. The academic buildings are arranged in a cluster that evokes the vitality of North Lebanon's villages. In assessing the master plan, University president Dr. Elie Salem has noted, "I am grateful for the love and care with which Sasaki has dealt with the University of Balamand."

Sasaki Associates, Inc.

Colorado College
Western Ridge Student Residences
Colorado Springs, Colorado

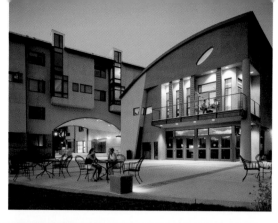

Right: Café Plaza.

Below: Gateway.

Bottom left: Aerial view.

Bottom right: Mountain vista.

Photography: Greg Hursley (exterior, interior), Alex S. MacLean (aerial).

The stunning backdrop for Colorado College—Pikes Peak and the Rocky Mountains—comes naturally for the only liberal arts and sciences college in Colorado Springs. Faculty and students take advantage of the region by studying geology in the Grand Canyon or anthropology in Anasazi ruins, and enjoying such pastimes as rock-climbing, skiing or tutoring local school children. But location is not the school's only distinction, as demonstrated by the new, 136,418-square foot, 283-bed Western Ridge Student Residences, designed by Sasaki Associates. The four handsome, freestanding dormitories, which help define the school's western boundary, substantially increase the number of students living on campus. Involving students in campus life is a keystone of Colorado College, where a student body of less than 2,000 under-graduates enjoys a high degree of personal attention from a dedicated faculty. The design of the Western Ridge Student Residences is no less inspiring, offering apartments that span the widths of the buildings for cross-ventilation and daylighting. Provided are such amenities as double-height living and dining spaces, full kitchens, compartmented baths, storage closets, single and double bedrooms for each four-student household, plus a Commons Room and a Café Plaza serving all residents. For a college founded in 1874 by visionary academicians, the new Residences seem to have reached another Rocky Mountain high.

165

Sasaki Associates, Inc.

University of California, Berkeley
New Century Plan
Berkeley, California

Left: Campus vista featuring Sather Tower or Campanile.

Right: Analysis Diagrams.

Lower right: Plan of UC Berkeley's 1,232-acre campus.

Illustration:
Sasaki Associates, Inc.

California's Gold Rush had captured public attention in 1849, when the State Constitution's drafters required the legislature to "encourage by all suitable means the promotion of intellectual, scientific, moral and agricultural improvement" among California's citizens. Even then, these visionaries dreamed of a university which, "if properly organized and conducted, would contribute even more than California's gold to the glory and happiness of advancing generations." Twenty years later, the University of California was chartered on 160 acres of land north of Oakland that was named

Berkeley—the first of many campuses—and has kept growing since. The 21st century finds UC Berkeley at the threshold of major physical change, for which Sasaki Associates has developed the New Century Plan. Responding to the growing number of college-age Californians and the need to upgrade the seismic safety of existing buildings, the New Century Plan guides the University in optimizing the use of land and capital. It preserves the legacy of landscape and architecture, and improves the quality of campus life.

Sasaki Associates, Inc.

Evergreen Valley College Performing/Visual Arts Center
San Jose, California

The new 68,000-square foot Performing/Visual Arts Center, designed by Sasaki Associates, will mark another milestone for Evergreen Valley College, a thriving public community college founded in 1975 on a picturesque, 175-acre site in San Jose's eastern foothills. Three buildings will constitute the Center: the Arts Building, including a lecture hall, art studios, an outdoor sculpture studio, a foundry, a jewelry classroom and a graphics laboratory; the Music Building, including a choral performance room, music practice rooms, classrooms, a library, a conference room and administrative offices; and the Theatre Building, including a 450-seat performance hall, a 125-seat back box theater, dance studio, a theater support room and an exhibition gallery. Together, they will welcome students from the San Jose/Evergreen Community College District to lessons—and possibly careers—in the arts.

Above left: Pedestrian bridge joining the music building with the theatre building.

Above right: View from adjoining road.

Right: View from campus center.

Illustration:
Sasaki Associates, Inc.

Sasaki Associates, Inc.

Cleveland State University
Recreation Center
Cleveland, Ohio

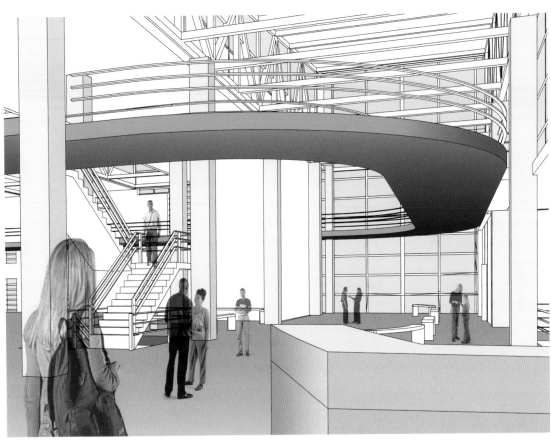

Upper right: Principal elevation.

Above: Atrium and indoor running track.

Below: Sidewalk perspective.

Illustration: Sasaki Associates, Inc.

By emphasizing its accessibility, urban focus, and strong faculty research and publications, Cleveland State University has played an important role in Cleveland. It is proud to be the State of Ohio's most diverse public institution and a national and state leader in graduating minority students from graduate and professional programs. The design of its Recreation Center, now in construction, typifies its progressive outlook. Besides expanding the athletic activities for students beyond those in the existing and adjoining Physical Education building, the new, 126,000-square foot, three-story Recreation Center, designed by Sasaki Associates in association with Weber Murphy Cox as architect of record, serves as a showcase for student recruitment. An atrium between the new space and the old accommodates a public bridge through the Center. Pedestrians traveling between a parking garage and the core of the campus as well as people on the sidewalk, can experience the activity within the Center while remaining separate from it. The image of openness complements the Center's expanses of glass and its spatial organization of large, open spaces that flow into each other without dedicated corridors. Simultaneously, it portrays the racquet sport courts, double gymnasium, indoor running track, weights and fitness facilities, multi-activity court, juice bar, locker rooms, day care facility and underground parking as a dynamic resource and potent symbol.

Shepley Bulfinch Richardson and Abbott

40 Broad Street
Boston, MA 02109-4306
617.423.1700
617.451.2420 (Fax)
www.sbra.com

Shepley Bulfinch Richardson and Abbott

Shepley Bulfinch Richardson and Abbott

Princeton University
Marquand Library of Art and Archaeology
Princeton, New Jersey

Outside, the transformation is subtle at Princeton University's Marquand Library of Art and Archaeology, a Brutalist modern building originally designed by Steinmann Cain & White in 1966. However, when Shepley Bulfinch Richardson and Abbott recently remodeled 29,000 square feet of existing space in the facility and added 17,000 square feet of new construction, the architect invested the interior with a new openness and sense of identity to foster multiple ways of learning and create fresh opportunities for scholarly collaboration—all without disturbing the existing modern exterior. Three principal design elements have contributed to the transformation of the library, which includes 109 carrels and is heavily used by graduate students, professors, visiting scholars and undergraduates. The addition of a penthouse with study carrels and seminar rooms on the third level brings a new "prospect," further increasing the transparency throughout the library. In addition, all levels of the building afford broad views of the campus. The renovation of the reading spaces, book stacks, classrooms, group study rooms, administrative offices and staff processing areas on the first and second levels enhances scholarship in its many forms. Finally, the expansion of the below-grade level introduces space for compact shelving and a skylit "refuge" for reading tables and carrels. The completed project includes the introduction of attractive, fully-wired spaces with richly stained woodwork, glass interior walls, vibrant colors, a permanent installation of ancient mosaic panels from an archeological dig and such sturdy, practical yet comfortable furnishings as plug-and-play carrels. Attendance at Marquand increased by 86 percent in its first seven months to more than 146,200 users.

Top: Exterior at dusk.

Above: Library instruction room.

Right: Lower level reading room.

Opposite top: Third level reading area.

Opposite right: Circulation area.

Opposite far right: Second level reading area.

Photography: Peter Mauss/ESTO.

Shepley Bulfinch Richardson and Abbott

Boston College
Higgins Hall
Chestnut Hill, Massachusetts

Past and present coexist everywhere on the Collegiate Gothic campus of Boston College, one of America's oldest Jesuit Catholic universities. It was founded in 1863 and serves 8,900 undergraduate and 4,700 graduate students. A remarkable example of this juxtaposition is Higgins Hall, a physics and biology building built in 1968 where a new, award-winning 120,000-square foot renovation and 110,000-square foot expansion designed by Shepley Bulfinch

Richardson and Abbott has created a modern, dynamic and interactive environment for research and teaching. With land scarce, the new construction has been integrated into the existing structure on the sloping site, replacing a Modernist exterior with a Gothic-style one. The relationship between the new and old structures conceals a dramatic surprise: a light-filled, five-story atrium symbolic of the "spaces within spaces" that have made Higgins Hall a superb place for scientific

work and spirited dialogue among faculty, undergraduates and graduate students. Says Physics Department chairman Kevin Bedell, "This is really a model for science teaching and research space because it has created an entirely different culture."

Above left: Skylighted atrium viewed from lunch room.

Above right: Spiral staircase between facility floors.

Upper right: Flexible laboratory bench.

Top right: Biology laboratory.

Opposite: Atrium during a conference.

Photography: Richard Mandelkorn.

Shepley Bulfinch Richardson and Abbott

Illinois Wesleyan University
Hansen Student Center
Bloomington, Illinois

Right: Main entrance.

Below left: Tommy's pub.

Below right: Bookstore facade.

Opposite above: Centre Court.

Opposite below: Entrance lobby.

Photography: Peter Aaron/ ESTO Photographics.

You can still hear lively student voices at Illinois Wesleyan University's former Memorial Gymnasium. Today, however, the Neo-Classical 1920s landmark on the Bloomington, Illinois campus has become the vibrant, new, 33,000-square foot, three-story Hansen Student Center. Through the adaptive reuse renovation designed by Shepley Bulfinch Richardson and Abbott, students come here for such amenities as a two-story bookstore, café, information center, offices for student government and other student organizations, conference rooms, newsstand, and a pub with an outdoor patio. The award-winning facility is the first of its kind for the independent, highly-rated school founded in 1850, and student participation was crucial to its development. Speaking of students' goals for Hansen Center, James Matthews, dean of students at Illinois Wesleyan, recalls, "They wanted non-institutional space, as wide a variety of spaces as possible, flexibility in potential use of all spaces and a building that offered students' choices for programming." The key to the project was transforming the existing first floor basketball court into a classic "black box theater" with flexible sound, lighting and structural systems derived from theater design, and inserting a mezzanine with a curving balcony in the double-height space to create an informal amphitheater. The space beneath the arc of the mezzanine was enclosed with store fronts to define an indoor "street," and the mezzanine was fitted out for campus organizations' offices. With recent stagings of such popular events as a film series, musicals, concerts, guest lectures and even a late night final exam study hall, Hansen Center has been transformed from a Neo-Classical gymnasium to a classic student center.

Shepley Bulfinch Richardson and Abbott

Brooklyn College/City University of New York
Brooklyn College Library
Brooklyn, New York

Below left: Existing Library and new addition. (Albert Vecerka/ESTO)

Below right: Reading room. (Peter Aaron/ESTO)

Below middle right: Media Center. (Peter Aaron/ESTO)

Bottom right: Reference area. (Peter Aaron/ ESTO)

Photography: Peter Aaron/ ESTO and Albert Vecerka /ESTO

One of 17 colleges of the City University of New York, Brooklyn College has been Brooklyn's premier institution of higher education since its founding in 1930. Now, the expansion and renovation by Shepley Bulfinch Richardson and Abbott, of LaGuardia Hall, a 1930s Georgian library building, and the Gideonese Addition, an adjoining 1950s structure, reestablishes LaGuardia Hall as Brooklyn College Library's main entrance. Additionally, it embellishes the Library's presence on the College's central quadrangle. The project adds 105,000 new square feet and renovates 170,000 square feet of existing space. The new library accommodates new functions supported by updated infrastructure and technology, and fully restores historic areas such as LaGuardia Hall's Main Reading Room. Old and new are integrated so seamlessly that Barbra Buckner Higginbotham, chief librarian of Brooklyn College, proudly declares, "The new Brooklyn College Library embodies both tradition and tomorrow, preserving our heritage while advancing our future."

Steven Ehrlich Architects

10865 Washington Boulevard
Culver City, California 90232
310.838.9700
310.838.9737 (Fax)
www.s-ehrlich.com
inquire@s-ehrlich.com

Steven Ehrlich Architects

Orange Coast College
Art Center
Costa Mesa, California

Southern California's beautiful beaches are just four miles away, but for over 25,000 students at Orange Coast College, in Costa Mesa, California, the focus is on their studies. Since some attend college and hold jobs at the same time, it,s fitting that Orange Coast, one of America,s largest single campus community colleges, was founded in 1948 on a deactivated World War II military base. Yet humble birth has not prevented the college from developing exceptional facilities, installing advanced computer and high-tech equipment, attracting a capable faculty, and enrolling a lively and diverse student body.

(About 55 percent of the students are Caucasian, 26 percent Asian, 15 percent Hispanic, two percent African American and one percent Native American.) In fact, among Orange Coast's 130-plus academic and career programs are such unexpected offerings as a School of Sailing and Seamanship, located five miles from the campus on Newport Bay in Newport Beach, and the recently completed, 65,000-square foot, three-story Art Center, a handsome structure designed by Steven Ehrlich Architects. The Art Center answers the college's fervent wish to unite the various components of the art department, which were scattered across campus. Not only does

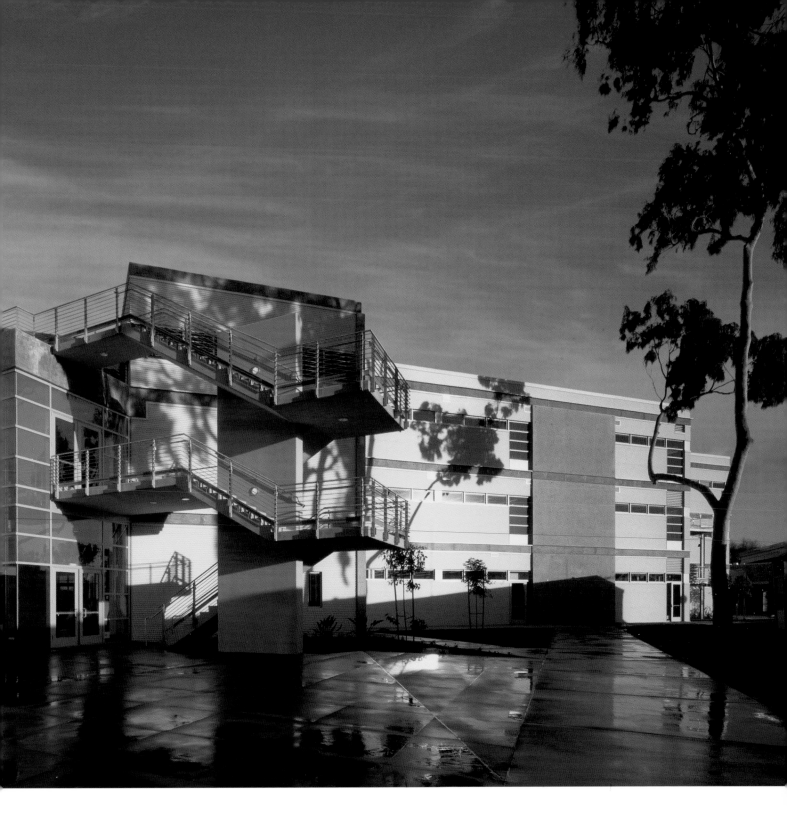

Steven Ehrlich Architects

the new facility pull the fine arts and commercial arts into a single building, it provides public gallery space, reconciles the 45-degree orientation of the campus with the orthogonal system of the city,s grid, and articulates an engaging, tripartite composition that visually expresses the distinctions between art disciplines. In an informal gesture to the human body, the "head" of the Art Center is represented by a dramatic, two-story entry volume sited on a quadrangle, where its transparent and welcoming steel and glass facade houses faculty offices and support spaces. The "torso" is a three-story, cast-in-place concrete building with a skin of corrugated metal siding and a ribbon clerestory window infill, where classrooms and studios are bisected by a full height, sky-lit atrium that encourages interaction among the multiple art disciplines. A one-story, steel industrial "shed" for heavy industrial processes completes the Art Center's form by bestowing a lithe and sinewy "limb."

Above: Atrium bridges to classrooms and studios.

Left: Pottery studio.

Below left: Exterior of industrial "shed."

Opposite: Perspective of atrium in classroom and studio building.

Steven Ehrlich Architects

University of California, Los Angeles
Kinross Staging Building
Los Angeles, California

Like the restless city it mirrors, the University of California, Los Angeles has grown dramatically ince its founding. What was designated the southern branch of the University of California in 1919 has evolved into a leading academic center serving 25,328 undergraduate students, 12,166 graduate students and 3,238 faculty members on a 419-acre campus in the city's Westwood Village district. World-class education, research and public service place heavy demands on the 160-plus campus buildings, however. Because many of these structures need seismic and technological upgrades, the university has developed the versatile, 75,000-square foot, three-story Kinross Staging Building designed by Stevenn Ehrlich Architects, as a temporary home in a permanent building for departments displaced by the renovation and upgrading of their original facilities. The flexible classroom, laboratory and arts building, a steel structure faced in CMU block at its front facade and steel and glass on its rear 2/3rds, is sited at the southern end of a 1-1/2 acre site. The project deftly reconciles creativity with

Above left: Detail of south facade.

Above: North facade and west elevation.

Opposite: Stair hall of gravity-resisting steel and shear-resisting masonry.

Photography: Grant Mudford.

fiscal and scheduling constraints. For example, its three section are separated by CMU walls that act as fire separation walls and waive the normally required fire rating, reducing costs, while its structural, mechanical and electrical systems are exposed, accommodating tenant improvements. The building's strategic importance was highlighted by the prompt arrival of its first tenants, World Arts and Culture and the Arts Department, for what should be a typical two-year tenure.

Top: Fascia of masonary contrasted with stell and glass.

Above left: Opening of ground floor to outdoor support yards.

Above right: Ground level space with glazes roll up doors.

Photography: Grant Mudford.

SWA Group

2200 Bridgeway
PO Box 5904
Sausalito, CA 94966
415.332.0719
451.332.0719 (Fax)
www.swa.com

SWA Group

Stanford University
Palo Alto, California

Directly below: Aerial view of Oval, Main Quad and a campus that has expanded beyond its founders' imagination.

Bottom: Projects that renew and affirm the original master planning concept.

Opposite: New/renovated Historic Courtyard.

Photography: Tom Fox.

In 1892, a year after the opening of Stanford University, Andrew D. White, president of Cornell University, toured the campus and commented, "When the entire plan is carried out, not even Oxford or Cambridge will have anything more beautiful." Many agreed. The great university established by railroad tycoon and former governor of California Leland Stanford and his wife Jane in memory of their only child, Leland Jr., arose on their 8,000-acre farm south of San Francisco with Shepley, Rutan & Coolidge as building architect and Frederick Law Olmsted as land planner and landscape architect. SWA Group has been working with Stanford for over 20 years to reclaim the campus's founding vision. Integrating Stanford's facility needs with a long-term landscape vision, SWA's varied projects are recovering the historic campus axes, quadrangles, view corridors and juxtaposition of formal landscaping with naturalistic landscapes within the central campus, while providing master planning for the 340-acre athletic grounds. Stanford's extraordinary campus has been reborn.

SWA Group   Soka University of America
Aliso Viejo, California

Even in California, which became the nation's most populous state in the years following World War II, developing a new campus from raw land to minimize site disturbance and appear complete at the opening was a tall order. Nevertheless, Japan-based Soka Gakkai International, one of the world's largest lay Buddhist organizations, achieved its goal by opening a fully accredited liberal arts university on a 103-acre campus for 1,500 undergraduate students in Orange County's Aliso Viejo (another campus serves graduate studies in

Calabassas), with Hardy Holzman Pfeiffer Associates as the architect and SWA Group as landscape architect. As a result, Soka University of America combines the Mediterranean-style architecture of a picturesque academic village with the landscaping of a Tuscan hill town. The 75-acre central campus, which overlooks Aliso and Wood Canyons Regional Park, is especially noteworthy for the way SWA has bolstered its ambitious design with a philosophy of ecological sustainability. A compact development envelope, for

example, minimizes site disturbance, maximizes pedestrian circulation and reduces the impact of utility installation, allocating over half the site to natural areas, open space and plantings that feature indigenous species, especially native oaks. In addition, building placement minimizes the need for mechanical air handling and electric lighting, parking acreage incorporates curbless edges and water filtering swales, and the steep existing topography is preserved by setting the buildings into terraced hillsides with overlooks and

view terraces. Phase I buildings, comprising three academic buildings, library, dining hall, eight residential buildings, student services building and gallery, gymnasium and four other non-academic buildings, will be augmented as the University reaches its build-out goal of facilities for 2,500 students. Meanwhile, areas planned for future phases have orchard plantings, which will sustain the sense of wholeness as the Soka University landscape ripens under the California sun.

Left: Lily-pond court at academic core.

Below left: Overlook on Aliso and Wood Canyons.

Below right: Banked slope of cobbles forms lake edge.

Bottom: Academic core of library, student center and dean's and president's buildings.

Opposite: Densely clustered residential buildings hug terraced hillsides.

Photography: Tom Fox, Lilia Schnaas.

SWA Group

Tokyo University of Foreign Studies
Fuchu, Japan

A thriving offspring of prestigious Tokyo University recently opened in an unlikely place--a former military base on the outskirts of Tokyo. Tokyo University of Foreign Studies, which conducts undergraduate and graduate programs on world languages, cultures and societies, and international relations, occupies a 30-acre site in Fuchu that SWA Group has composed as a clear, hierarchical landscape. Part of the scheme's strength resides in its sense of progression. Visitors arriving from the town's retail center and transit station follow a formal sequence of spaces that takes them from an entry plaza along a diagonal spine to a central plaza, the academic heart of the campus, before proceeding to interconnected courtyards and gardens that end in the student housing and playing fields. However, the campus also boasts more mature trees than its age would merit, because half of its existing mature trees were set aside and replanted after the site was regraded for drainage and seismic reasons, and buildings were positioned to preserve as many additional standing trees as possible. And the absence of cars and trucks establishes a human scale everywhere, including the open spaces, where people meet, study and read, and the two-story perimeter walkway connecting buildings on the central plaza. The transition from military base to campus is 80 percent complete after just five years of development.

Above left and right: Garden for reading and grove in central plaza.

Right: Pyramidal landscape feature in the courtyard.

Below left and right: Perimeter walkway frames the central plaza and the interactive fountain.

Opposite: Conical landscape feature.

Photography: Tom Fox.

SWA Group

Cy-Fair College
Cypress, Texas

Under a tight schedule to finish construction before classes began in August 2003, Cy-Fair College, the newest addition to the North Harris Montgomery Community College District, in Harris County, Texas, recorded a dramatic advance with the installation of its landscaping. As consultant to Gensler, the architect of the college, SWA Group provided master planning and landscape architectural design to prepare the 200-acre campus to receive over 10,000 students, and identified two critically important issues that would decisively shape the overall campus design. First, the need to detain

and retain storm water led SWA to design a campus-wide lake system that would immediately became the focal point for the College's buildings. Second, native Katy prairie grass was incorporated into the landscape design, a positive step in preserving this valuable but rapidly disappearing asset. For a practical-minded institution offering students a quality education, affordability, smaller classes and modern facilities, Cy-Fair's stately buildings, broad expanses of water and lush prairie grass meadows have created a memorable campus.

Above, left, and right: Walkway and plaza.

Left: Cascade helps drain lake system.

Photography: Tom Fox.

William Wilson Associated Architects Inc.

374 Congress Street
Suite 400
Boston, MA 02210
617.338.5990
617.338.5991 (Fax)
www.wilsonarch.com
info@wilsonarch.com

William Wilson Associated Architects Inc.

William Wilson Associated Architects Inc.

Tulane University
Merryl and Sam Israel, Jr.
Environmental Sciences Building
New Orleans, Louisiana

Above: Laboratory benches and exhaust hoods.

Left: Elevation facing historic Front Quadrangle.

Below left: Laboratory windows.

Opposite: Open walkways connecting Israel Building and existing Stern Hall.

Photography: Brian Vanden Brink.

"Science is fun," says Dr. Gary McPherson, associate dean of arts & sciences for Tulane University. "It's especially fun when researchers have spacious, modern, clean and safe laboratories to conduct scientific exploration." McPherson refers to the new, 50,000-square foot, four-story Merryl and Sam Israel, Jr. Environmental Sciences Building, designed by William Wilson Associated Architects with Payette Associates, on the 110-acre Uptown campus of Tulane University in New Orleans. The opening of the Israel Building marks another milestone for one of America's leading private research institutions, founded in 1834. 7,862 undergraduates and 5,114 graduate and professional students are currently enrolled. Besides supporting Tulane's ongoing environmental research, the new facility is built with recycled materials and equipped with energy conservation features. Of course, the design reflects state-of-the-art technology, from the undergraduate chemistry labs on the bottom and top floors to the laboratory space and offices for cell and molecular biologists, ecology and evolutionary biologists, environmental engineers and other researchers on the middle two floors. The laboratories are also open and light-filled, unlike those in adjacent Stern Hall, the primary campus science building, to which the new structure is connected by open walkways on upper floors and a palm-tree patio on the ground. If students like working in the Israel Building, so does faculty — making its laboratory space a prized assignment.

William Wilson Associated Architects Inc.

Hood College
Hodson Science and Technology Center
Frederick, Maryland

Right: Elevation facing new Science Quadrangle.

Below left: Laboratory.

Below right: Laboratory.

Opposite: Atrium.

Photography: Anton Grassl.

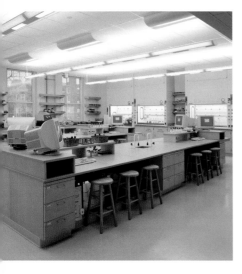

Founded in 1893 and noted for its beautiful campus of classical architecture in the historic city of Frederick, Maryland, Hood College routinely combines the contemporary needs of 1,693 students and 100 faculty members with a proud tradition as a small, coeducational, intellectual community. Thus, the recent opening of the new Hodson Science and Technology Center, a modern, 80,000-square foot laboratory facility in a stately, Neo-Georgian building, designed by William Wilson Associated Architects, has quietly enhanced the august image of the 50-acre campus. The development encompasses 50,000 square feet of new construction. Included are undergraduate teaching and research laboratories, a 50-seat classroom, three-story atrium, faculty offices and social spaces, forming a new science quadrangle. There is, as well, 30,000 square feet of renovation to the existing Hodson Science Hall, resulting in new laboratory, classroom and office space. What makes the Center truly outstanding, however, is the close relationship between classroom and laboratory, allowing students to integrate their laboratory and lecture experiences and permitting faculty to include students at all levels of advanced scientific research. Dr. Craig Laufer, associate professor of biology at Hood, happily observes, "What you will find are comfortable places for students and faculty to interact, modest research spaces just perfect for faculty and student to work together, and classrooms of a size that are conducive to the give-and-take between instructor and student that are the strength of the Hood education."

William Wilson Associated Architects Inc.

Vanderbilt University
BioSciences/Medical Research Building III
Nashville, Tennessee

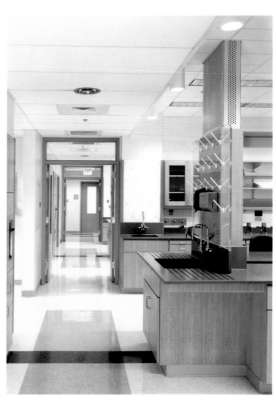

Making vital connections has been the story of Vanderbilt University since 19th-century tycoon Commodore Cornelius Vanderbilt decided at age 79 to donate the $1 million gift that founded the school in Nashville in the spring of 1873. From the moment that Methodist Bishop Holland N. McTyeire, a cousin of the Commodore's young second wife, won the Commodore's support for building a university in the South to "contribute to strengthening the ties which should exist between all sections of our common country," Vanderbilt has grown

from a 75-acre campus for 307 students in 1875 to a 313-acre campus for 10,885 undergraduates and graduate and professional students. In this spirit of unity, the completion of the new, 350,000-square foot, nine-story BioSciences/ Medical Research Building III, designed by William Wilson Associated Architects, establishes a vital, pro-grammatic link between the college of Arts & Sciences at Vanderbilt University and Vanderbilt University Medical Center. The building incorporates an existing 85,000-square foot structure into the

Above left: Atrium.

Above right: North elevation detail.

Below right: Research laboratory.

Oppposite: North elevation detail.

Photography: Anton Grassl.

198

William Wilson Associated Architects Inc.

Left: Lecture hall.

Below: Teaching laboratory.

new construction and extends multi-level connections to six other existing facilities, introducing a nine-story atrium with an open staircase and casual seating areas to mediate the differences in new and existing floor heights. It also provides daylight and a social core where students and faculty can congregate. The link is completed by stacking the occupants of the building so that Medical School research is co-located with related Arts & Sciences research, mixing people from similar fields in the Medical School and the University on each floor. Thus, the four teaching laboratories, 64 research laboratories, 8,650-square foot greenhouse, 118-seat lecture hall, faculty offices, conference rooms, glasswash/autoclave rooms, atrium and new loading dock represent more than a state-of-the-art showcase for teaching and research. As Vanderbilt's chancellor Joseph B. Wyatt declares, "This research facility is unique. It is a building designed from its first concept to encourage diverse research disciplines to share resources, facilities, ideas and discoveries."

creating better environments

Concerned about the Indoor Air Quality in your School?

flax

pine rosin

wood flour & jute

Marmoleum Elementary addresses the needs of educational facility managers who are faced with the challenge of improving the indoor air quality of their schools, while reducing operating costs.

Made from readily renewable natural ingredients, Marmoleum Elementary has naturally occurring antistatic and antimicrobial properties, making it not only hygienic and easy to clean, but also an aid in the reduction of indoor air pollutants. What's more, Marmoleum Elementary is one of the lowest cost maintenance floors available. These features combined with unmatched durability, unlimited design possibilities and one of the quietest underfoot resilient floors available, make Marmoleum Elementary the ideal choice for classrooms, corridors and cafeterias in any school.

Forbo Flooring
Humboldt Industrial Park
P.O. Box 667
Hazleton, PA 18201
phone: 570-459-0771/1-800-842-7839
fax: 570-450-0258
e-mail: info@fL-NA.com
www.forboLinoleumNA.com

MARMOLEUM® ELEMENTARY

Testing, Testing . . .

By Roger Yee

While no one knows how the ideal environment for America's schools should be designed, intriguing ideas are being proposed—and built—to prepare students for a brave new world.

Henry Ford's daring announcement in 1914 that he would set the minimum wage for employees at Ford Motor Company's Highland Park, Michigan plant at $5 a day may not have single-handedly inaugurated middle class life in America. However, turning Ford employees into Ford customers had profound implications for American society: Workers could make a good living with just a high school education. This middle class reverie was rudely jolted in the late 1980s by successful competitors from foreign nations that educated their people, empowered them with capital and technology—just as America had done—and achieved equally impressive results.

Today, U.S. assembly-line workers who once considered themselves well paid and indispensable feel undervalued and expendable, as their jobs migrate to Mexico, Canada and destinations far beyond NAFTA's reach. To make matters worse, the high-technology jobs that were supposed to represent America's economic future are being outsourced as well. Ironically, the bright, young scientists, engineers and mathematicians of such nations as India, Russia and China, who previously regarded America as the land of golden opportunity, are now being wooed by American employers for jobs in their native lands. Higher education is more critical to America's survival than ever, and the public openly acknowledges this.

Trouble is, America's children may not be getting the right education for a working world where physical might continues to yield to brain power. Our well-known optimism about our children is not fully justified by the test scores that are now so critical to the Bush administration's key education initiative, the No Child Left Behind Act of 2001. (The legislation uses test scores to hold schools accountable for results, implement new programs based on scientific research, expand parental options, and broaden local control and flexibility.)

What's happening to America's lead in education?

Take the results of the 2003 National Assessment of Educational Progress (called "The Nation's Report Card"), conducted by the Department of Education. According to the NAEP, only 31 percent of 9-year-olds and 32 percent of 13-year-olds read at the level of proficiency or above, while just 32 percent of 9-year-olds and 29 percent of 13-year-olds scored in mathematics at the level of proficiency or above. If parents are anxious about their jobs going abroad, they should regard their children's difficulties in reading and mathematics as an early warning signal.

Indeed, American students' current world ranking could be described as mediocre. The latest Trends in International Math and Science Study, the most rigorous and comprehensive study of mathematics and science education in the United States and other nations, shows American eighth graders performed slightly better than the international average, 19th in mathematics and 18th in science out of 38 countries. Unfortunately, there is little evidence of long-term improvement to lift their scores into the upper ranks now dominated by nations like Singapore, South Korea, Taiwan and Japan, even though mathematics and science will strongly shape the global economy of the 21st century.

As if all this were not enough, more problems lie ahead for U.S. students seeking higher education, because their families are finding college and graduate school harder than ever to afford. Not only is public and private tuition rising faster than median family income, but state and federal aid for higher education is being cut rather than increased, students are taking longer to finish college so their families can save enough to cover tuition costs, student debt has doubled in the last decade, and fewer lower-income families

Society for College and University Planning . . .

Helping You Plan for Higher Education's Future

The Society for College and University Planning (SCUP) is the recognized leader in advancing the knowledge and practice of planning in higher education.

SCUP has nearly 5,000 higher education professionals worldwide interested in planning at all levels and in all contexts. SCUP's mission is to provide higher education professionals with planning knowledge, resources, and connections to achieve institutional goals.

Visit **www.scup.org** for information on how to join this growing community.

If your job involves planning, SCUP can help:

Academic planning
Campus planning
Capital planning
Community relations
Enrollment management
Facility planning
Financial planning
Institutional research planning
IT or technology planning
Master planning
Open spaces
Policy and governance
Space management planning
Strategic planning
Student housing planning
Student services/life planning

Contact SCUP

Contact us at **www.scup.org** for a wealth of frequently updated information and links.

SCUP Society for College and University Planning
339 East Liberty Street • Suite 300
Ann Arbor, Michigan 48104 USA
Phone: 734.998.7832
Fax: 734.998.6532
Email: membership@scup.org

Knock On Wood?

raleigh range

Bound by superstitions, like relying on wood? Our advanced polymer technology promises **low maintenance** products with the comforts of home. Fire-retardant, scratch-resistant and waterproof, our durable, modern furniture thrives in the challenging educational environment. Our products preserve internal air quality, and can be fully recycled. Can't see the wood for the trees? Think Duracase.

DURACASE®

A Duragroup Company
1.800.405.3441
www.duragroup.com

DURA FRAME by *Kwalu* · DURA CASE

Project Index